Contemporary British Muslim Arts and Cultural Production

I0472903

This unique collaboration between scholars, practitioners and Muslim artists profiles emerging forms of contemporary British Muslim art, prompting a debate about its purpose and its inclusion in UK society. It features analysis of Muslim art as a category, as well as reflective accounts of people working in theatre, popular music, the heritage sector and ancient and modern visual arts, often at the margins of the British arts industry.

Dealing with sociological and theological themes as well as art history and practice, the volume provides a timely intervention on a neglected topic. The collection discusses diverse topics including how second- and third-generation British Muslims, as part of a broader generational shift, have reworked Sufi music and traditional calligraphy and fused them with new musical and artistic styles, from Grime to comic book art, alongside consideration of the experiences of Muslim artists who work in the theatre, museums and the performing arts sectors.

It is a must-read for students and researchers of theology and religious studies, Islamic studies, fine art, cultural studies and ethnic and racial studies.

Sadek Hamid is a Research Fellow at the University of Wales Trinity St David.

Stephen H. Jones is a Lecturer in the Department of Theology and Religion, University of Birmingham.

Islam in the World
Series Editors: Katherine Brown and Jorgen Nielsen
Birmingham University, UK

Freedom of Speech in Universities
Islam, Charities and Counter-terrorism
Alison Scott-Baumann and Simon Perfect

Rivals in the Gulf
Yusuf al-Qaradawi, Abdullah Bin Bayyah, and the Qatar-UAE Contest
Over the Arab Spring and the Gulf Crisis
David H. Warren

Al-Ghazālī and the Idea of Moral Beauty
Sophia Vasalou

The Sharia Inquiry, Religious Practice and Muslim Family Law in Britain
Edited by Samia Bano

Contemporary British Muslim Arts and Cultural Production
Identity, Belonging and Social Change
Edited by Sadek Hamid and Stephen H. Jones

For more information and a full list of titles in the series, please visit:
https://www.routledge.com/Islam-in-the-World/book-series/ITWF

Contemporary British Muslim Arts and Cultural Production

Identity, Belonging and Social Change

Edited by Sadek Hamid and Stephen H. Jones

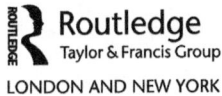

LONDON AND NEW YORK

First published 2023
by Routledge
4 Park Square, Milton Park, Abingdon, Oxon OX14 4RN

and by Routledge
605 Third Avenue, New York, NY 10158

*Routledge is an imprint of the Taylor & Francis Group, an informa
business*

British Library Cataloguing-in-Publication Data
A catalogue record for this book is available from the British Library

Library of Congress Cataloguing-in-Publication Data
Names: Hamid, Sadek, editor. | Jones, Stephen H., 1981- editor.
Title: Contemporary British Muslim arts and cultural production :
identity, belonging and social change / edited by Sadek Hamid and
Stephen H. Jones.
Description: 1. | New York : Routledge, 2023. | Series: Islam in the
world focus ; vol 5 | Includes bibliographical references and index. |
Identifiers: LCCN 2023005064 | ISBN 9781032362021 (hardback) |
ISBN 9781032362038 (paperback) | ISBN 9781003330714 (ebook)
Subjects: LCSH: Islamic art--Great Britain. | Islamic art--21st
century.
Classification: LCC N6768.65.I85 C66 2023 | DDC 704/.08
82970941--dc23/eng/20230412
LC record available at https://lccn.loc.gov/2023005064

ISBN: 978-1-032-36202-1 (hbk)
ISBN: 978-1-032-36203-8 (pbk)
ISBN: 978-1-003-33071-4 (ebk)

DOI: 10.4324/9781003330714

Typeset in Times New Roman
by MPS Limited, Dehradun

Contents

Preface and Acknowledgements   *vii*

List of Contributors   *ix*

Introduction   1

SADEK HAMID AND STEPHEN H. JONES

PART I

The Cultural Politics of British Muslim Artistic
Production   21

1 A British Muslim Arts Movement: Public Politics
   or Religious Devotion?   23
   CARL MORRIS

2 Decentring the Colonial Gaze: The Framing of
   Islamic Art   33
   SHAHEEN KASMANI

PART II

Art in Contemporary British Muslim Culture   49

3 The Nature of Islamic Art: Locating a Tradition
   of Fitrah in the Art and Culture of Islam, with
   Particular Reference to Calligraphy   51
   RAZWAN UL-HAQ

4   What is Post-*tariqa* Sufism?   58
    AYESHA KHAN

5   God and Grime: The Religious Literacy of British
    Hip-Hop   68
    ABDUL-AZIM AHMED

**PART III
The Inclusion of British Muslim Art**   81

6   The Playground for Dangerous Ideas: Muslims
    and British Theatre   83
    HASSAN MAHAMDALLIE

7   Arts, Heritage and Islamic Manuscripts   93
    NEELAM HUSSAIN

8   Flawed and Toxic? Challenges in Contemporary
    Islamic Art in the UK   109
    SARA CHOUDHREY

    Conclusion: The Future of British Muslim Arts   120
    SADEK HAMID AND STEPHEN H. JONES

    Index   *129*

Preface and Acknowledgements

Academics today frequently talk about the 'co-production' of research. By this, they usually mean the breaking down of barriers between researchers and researched, with non-academics having input in research questions or publications. Like many buzzwords in academia, co-production is more often talked about than done, but this book is a genuine attempt at putting these ideas into practice. It is the result of a collaboration between scholars, artists and curators – with many of the contributors to the volume occupying more than one of these identities at once. Some chapters contain scholarly analysis, while others take the view of artists themselves, with the authors writing of their experiences in the sector or how their beliefs shape their work. Readers will notice that style and standpoint shift markedly between chapters, but in a way that ultimately, we hope, provides a much richer insight into the Muslim arts scene in the UK. This is all the more the case because some contributors fundamentally dispute the terms and concepts we use.

Taking on a project like this involves various challenges and risks and we are grateful to the many people who have helped the project along the way. We would like to thank Mobeen Butt for the original inspiration and creative momentum behind this volume. We owe our thanks to many other current and former leaders of the Muslims in Britain Research Network (MBRN), notably Alison Scott-Baumann and Ayesha Khan, who helped organise the 'Exploring Contemporary Muslim Art, Culture and Heritage in Britain' conference. We also owe a debt to Carl Morris, who did much to transform MBRN from a scholarly network to an active collaboration between academics and communities.

We are grateful to all the contributors who patiently endured the delays and complications that can arise in the production of multi-author publications such as this, not least for staying committed through the difficult Covid-19 crisis. We thank Razwan ul-Haq, Sara Choudhrey and Shaheen Kasmani in particular for kindly allowing us to reproduce the images and artwork that accompany their chapters. Thanks are also due to the series editors, especially Katherine Brown, and Rebecca Clintworth, Ceri McLardy and Iman Hakimi at Routledge for agreeing to take this project on, for their enthusiasm during production and reviewing and ultimately for enabling this book to be in your hands.

Sadek Hamid and Stephen H. Jones

Contributors

Abdul-Azim Ahmed is Deputy Director of the Islam-UK Centre at Cardiff University. His research has focused on mosques, civil society and Islam in Wales. He has authored several journal articles including 'Thinking Congregationally About British Muslims' (*Journal of Islam and Christian–Muslim Relations*), 'Conceptualising Mosque Diversity' (*Journal of Muslims in Europe*) and is currently working on a monograph titled *The Contemporary British Mosque.*

Sara Choudhrey is a London-based artist researcher, exploring themes of space, place, heritage and identity. She conducts studies in art and design, referencing historical collections, archives and architecture. Sara raises the question of hybrid practice evolving in affinity with varied perspectives of art historical narratives. Her installation *Siraat* was recently shortlisted for the Aesthetica Art Prize 2022. Sara holds a Master's (UAL, 2010) and a PhD in Digital Arts (University of Kent, 2018).

Razwan ul-Haq is a QEST scholar (Queen Elizabeth Scholarship Trust; Royal Warrant Holders Association). He worked in senior management roles in schools before a career change led him to become a professional Artist, working primarily in Arabic calligraphy. As a child, he was inspired by his uncle Maulvi Fazal Azeem, who was a professional scribe, and now Razwan is one of only a handful of calligraphers practicing Nastaliq calligraphy using traditional materials in the UK. He has studied with masters such as Dr Nassar Mansour and Keramat Fathinia, and he has provided professional calligraphy services for the National Literacy Trust as well as producing calligraphy work for Leeds City Art Gallery, Ilkley Literature Festival and Bradford City of Culture 2025. He has also used his background in calligraphy to produce Land Art for the Tour de France and is a visiting lecturer at Cheltenham Ladies College and Ullswater College.

Sadek Hamid is a Research Fellow at the University of Wales Trinity St David. He has previously held teaching and research positions at the Universities of Chester, Liverpool Hope and Oxford University's Centre for Islamic Studies. He is the author of *Sufis, Salafis and Islamists: The Contested Ground of British Islamic Activism* (I.B Tauris, 2018), co-author of *British Muslims: New Directions in Islamic Thought, Creativity and Activism* (Edinburgh University Press, 2018), editor of *Young British Muslims: Between Rhetoric and Realities* (Routledge, 2016) and co-editor of *Youth Work and Islam: A Leap of Faith for Young People* (Sense, 2011) and *Political Muslims: Understanding Youth Resistance in a Global Context* (Syracuse University Press, 2018).

Neelam Hussain is the Curator of the Mingana Collection of Middle Eastern Manuscripts at the Cadbury Research Library, University of Birmingham. Much of her work involves research, teaching, exhibitions and public engagement on early Qur'an manuscripts and the material culture of Islamic manuscripts. In 2020, She helped establish the MIAH Foundation, which aims to increase the engagement of Muslim communities in the arts and cultural sector with the long-term aim to establish the UK's first museum dedicated to Islamic Arts and Heritage in Birmingham.

Stephen H. Jones is a sociologist of religion whose primary areas of expertise are in Islam and Muslims in the UK and religious and non-religious publics' perceptions of science. He is a Lecturer in the Department of Social Policy, Sociology and Criminology, University of Birmingham, and from 2017 to 2020 was General Secretary of the Muslims in Britain Research Network. He is the author of *Islam and the Liberal State* (I.B Tauris, 2021) and has published on themes including Muslim political representation, Islamophobia in the UK, multiculturalism in local government and preventing extremism policies.

Shaheen Kasmani is a specialist in surface pattern and textile design, principally using traditional patterns and motifs, in both conventional and contemporary contexts. Her background is in language, literature and education and has always had an interest and a love for the visual arts. A graduate of The Prince's School of Traditional Arts in London, she completed her MA in Visual Islamic Traditional Arts in 2014.

Ayesha Khan completed her PhD from Cardiff University in 2020. Her thesis explored contemporary Sufi expression amongst young British Muslims. Since completing her studies, she has since worked as a policy specialist and consultant in the public and private sectors. She has also founded her own policy and research charity, CareStart, where she bridges her experience to provide culturally sensitive support to communities.

Hassan Mahamdallie is a playwright and director. A former Director of the Muslim Institute, he is the Senior Editor on its journal *Critical Muslim*. Hassan is the founder of theatre company Dervish Productions. He writes on culture, working class and Black history and politics, racism and Islamophobia. He is the author of *Crossing the River of Fire: The Socialism of William Morris* (Redwords, 2008/2021).

Carl Morris is a Lecturer in Religion, Culture and Society at the University of Central Lancashire. His research sits at the intersection between the sociologies of religion and media, with a particular focus on Muslims in Britain. His recent book, *Muslims Making British Media* (Bloomsbury, 2022), examines Muslim cultural producers working in television, film, music, comedy, and theatre.

Introduction

Sadek Hamid and Stephen H. Jones

After more than 15 years of state securitisation, hostile media coverage and rising levels of Islamophobia, many Muslims in the UK express a widespread sense of being held 'under siege – spied on, interrogated, routinely asked to "put their house in order" as if they were not, and had never been, an equal part of British society'.[1] However, hysterical headlines, feelings of grievance and disempowerment are only a small part of the unfolding story of Islam in Britain. Against a broader backdrop of increasing scrutiny of, and prejudice towards, Muslims in the West, artistic expression has emerged as a means by which Muslim Britons contest their position and portrayal in society and tackle difficult subjects that have sometimes proven taboo within traditional community networks and institutions. It is an area that has received minimal media attention, in part because Muslim artists typically occupy the margins of the UK arts, culture and heritage sectors – an industry that, as this collection shows, often exhibits forms of structural racism and Islamophobia.

Despite these challenging circumstances, we are in living in a time of great global Muslim cultural creativity that has accelerated through the possibilities of digital technology and has enabled the emergence of a dynamic, creative class of Muslim Millennials – dubbed 'Generation M' – who are driving cultural shifts, consumption patterns and political change.[2] These younger Muslims are experimental in their approach to religious matters, are at the forefront of social transformative activism and synthesise their faith and ethnic backgrounds within the dominant norms of the societies in which they live. Their artistic tastes reflect the diasporic reinventions of tradition and hybrid manifestations of Islamically infused forms of art, music, material culture, theatre, architecture, poetry, literature and humour. These innovative creatives simultaneously represent a response to the global dominance of Western popular culture and the generational change taking place across Muslims in majority and minority contexts, as the youth demographic grows to produce distinctive Millennial and 'Generation Z' subcultures.

DOI: 10.4324/9781003330714-1

American female Muslim artist Zakiyyah Rahman for instance has stated that 'We realized young Muslims – especially sisters – needed to see that you can live a dope life and value your religion. That it is possible'.[3] This sentiment is indicative of the increasing 'Muslims speaking back' mood of young Western Muslims fusing their religious beliefs with their artistic ambition and challenging stereotypical perceptions of women in the public sphere through the medium of hip-hop music (see Chapter 5 in this volume). These counter-narratives take many forms and include a multitude of young people who draw inspiration from their African and Caribbean heritage and embrace new but authentic modern culture.[4] This parallels the experiences of Puerto Rican American Rap artist Hamza Perez, subject of the documentary *New Muslim Cool,* which follows his new life after conversion to Islam and use of music to spread faith among various urban Muslim communities in post-9/11 America.[5] He and other performers, such as Mos Def and Talib Kweli, have inspired a growing number of European Muslim bands who adopted conscious rap styles, to create political awareness and challenge racism and Islamophobia. In the UK, groups such as Mecca2Medina were the trailblazers of Islamised rap music and in turn helped to promote spoken word younger acts such as Poetic Pilgrimage – aka 'Hip-hop Hijabis'. The link between Islam and African American Muslim music and activism developed many decades ago (see Chapter 1 in this volume). Unknown to most people is the fact that early pioneers of jazz and rap music and some of the most famous hip-hop artists were either Muslims or utilised Islamic imagery and references in their lyrics.[6] This increasingly popular transatlantic intellectual, cultural and political exchange has been called the 'Muslim Atlantic', a shared linguistic, creative and cultural space that takes its inspiration from the influential book *The Black Atlantic: Modernity and Double Consciousness* by Paul Gilroy.[7] A shared language, popular culture, historical entanglements and similar experiences of racism, Islamophobia, securitisation and views of British and American foreign policy on the Muslim world built a 'special relationship' between the UK and US Muslims. These cultural ties are further strengthened by familial connections, personal friendships, public speakers and mutual admiration of towering iconic Black Muslims such as Muhammad Ali and Malcolm X. Both figures continue to be a source of inspiration, and Malcolm X's powerful story of personal journey of transformation and emancipation continues to inspire artistic and political influence on Hip-hop music, the Internet and Muslim community organisations in both Britain and America.[8]

Muslims and Islamicate Culture

Creating a 'culture' is generally regarded as the collective shaping of ideas, values, traditions, artistic practices and products which are ongoing processes that encompass the cumulative efforts and achievements of people who share an identity based upon a combination of religion, language, history and geography. Muslim artistic cultures are syncretic, drawing upon a variety of influences that are both religious and secular, historical and contemporary. This raises a variety of complex – and within Muslim communities, sometimes vigorously contested – definitional questions: What determines the difference between Islamic arts and arts produced by Muslims? And what does Islamic art mean for Islam?[9] The adjective 'Islamic' is normally used to describe personal and social behaviours inspired by the religious worldview of Islam. The phrase 'Islamic art' is suggestive of art and artefacts of Muslim origin, expression and usage. It may bring to mind dazzling geometric patterns, beautiful ceramics, ornate calligraphy, complex forms of manuscript illumination or a centuries-old Qur'an folio in a museum. The term was, in fact, initially coined by European art historians,[10] who used the term 'Islamic art' in a more secularised sense, to refer to 'Islam' as culture rather than religion.[11] Muslims themselves however – and more recently, some scholars of Islamic Art – are happier with a normative definition that would refer to the infusion of faith-based principles and pious practices across the sacred and mundane aspects of human interactions in Muslim life. The end result is the creation of material and cultural products that are recognisably shaped by teachings and religious values and traditions which manifest Quranic imperatives that celebrate the oneness of the Divine, unity of creation, achievement of virtue and cultivation of beauty.[12]

Historically, these values manifested in huge geographical variations across different Muslim cultures and traditions as a result of the encounters with the civilisational traditions of Persia, Mesopotamia, Africa, India and China. The successful historical spread of Islam is in part explained by its ability to remain a 'mobile idea' that was easily understood everywhere and flexible enough to merge 'in intriguing ways to produce unanticipated new configurations'.[13] Marshall G. Hodgson in his multi-volume book *The Venture of Islam* describes the product of this process as 'Islamicate' – the organic creation of culture in regions in which Muslims were culturally dominant but whose civilisational artefacts 'would refer not directly to the religion, Islam, itself, but to the social and cultural complex historically associated with Islam and the Muslims and even found among non-Muslims'.[14] In other words, Islamicate Art was made by Christians, Jews and people of other faiths. Even so, within the vast diversity of Muslim history, it is possible to identify an underlying commonality underpinned by a widely shared Islamic worldview. Artistic expression inspired by the religion of Islam is most often associated with calligraphy, geometric patterns and arabesques that display remarkable similarities across time and space.[15] Islamised art forms hold an aesthetic appeal to many non-Muslims despite the layers of religious symbolism contained within it and have shaped Western art from the ninth century to the present day.[16] Oludamini Ogunnaike, in his illuminating article *The Silent Theology of Islamic Art,* observes the strange irony of how the appetite for consuming Islamic arts and culture has not decreased in the face of increasing anti-Muslim attitudes across the world:

> [D]espite the dissemination of virulent propaganda against Islam in the West, many people from Western societies queue for hours to admire the architecture of the Alhambra in Spain and the Taj Mahal in India as well as exhibitions of Islamic calligraphy and miniature paintings, and to attend sold-out concerts of traditional Islamic music.[17]

Ogunnaike notes that scholars such as Seyyed Hossein Nasr and Titus Burckhardt discern an essence or universal Islamic approach rooted in sacred religious inspiration and not historical influences and cultural variations (see Chapters 2 and 3 in this volume). Nasr argues that Quranic calligraphy enjoys a special privilege in Islam as the visual embodiment of divine revelation, as 'the geometry of the spirit'.[18] In doing so, these scholars distinguish religiously inspired art from desacralised art made by Muslims who see their pursuit in entirely secular terms and create 'art for art's sake'.[19] In *Islam: The View from the Edge,* Richard Bulliet offers a typological frame to explain what he calls the territorial centres and edges of Islamic civilisation and suggests that 'the impetus for change in Islam has more often come from the bottom than from the top, from the edge than from the centre'.[20] He contends that the most innovative Muslim cultural production took place at the geographical periphery of Muslim lands than its political centre.

   Contemporary Muslim artistic expressions can be imperfectly categorised as either embodying the distinct aesthetic inspired by faith, alluded to above, or pursuing secular varieties of Muslim identity and creating art for art's sake. The latter may have recognisable references to cultures from Muslim societies but are, often on their own understanding, not necessarily 'Islamic' as they integrate ideas and imagery that would be considered inconsistent with the sensibilities of normative religious teaching. Many religiously committed Muslims, in the West and elsewhere, perceive a general moral decline in their societies and see challenges to their faith resulting from the impact of globalisation and secularisation that have redefined social norms. As Yolanda van Tilborgh notes, the development of Muslim art and culture in the early twentieth century has been 'shaped by experiences of colonialism, independence movements, the globalisation of Islam, and various ethnic, cultural and socio–political changes'.[21] Various reformist movements in the late twentieth century have attempted to re-Islamise their societies and produce forms of religiously inspired artistic culture in Muslim majority and minority contexts to contribute to a pan-Islamic revival. This was clearly visible in the Middle East and as alternative cultural forms such as 'halal songs', 'halal television soaps', 'clean cinema' and 'Islamic theatre' became available to those dissatisfied with Western cinema and TV and secularised cultural production generated in Muslim countries. This has been described as attempts to 'Islamise Modernity', while others have labelled these efforts as 'Modernising Islam'.[22]

Building present-day variants based upon tradition, however, is not a linear process and, for many contemporary Muslim artists, is seen as an ongoing journey that involves a process of negotiation of the relationships between the symbols and signs of the sacred and secular. French Algerian artist Kader Attia captured the difficulties succinctly when asked if there is such a thing as contemporary Islamic arts, he responded: 'I would answer, we are currently building it, re-appropriating (unconsciously) our culture and its influences in our own way'.[23] This reconstructive impulse has provoked fierce internal debates about what constitutes lawful arts, music and entertainment among religious scholars. There are various unresolved tensions about the (im)permissibility of the use of musical instruments to accompany the performance of songs, with the best-known illustration of this being the musician Yusuf Islam/Cat Stevens's rejection of, and then return to, his song-writing career. Disputes about the lawfulness of percussion instruments, other than the daff drum, are not new and have long been a source of scholarly debate.[24] Conservative Muslims, who take a hard-line 'legalistic' view, also argue that music should be largely forbidden because it arouses passions that are not religiously centred and destroy public morality. This continues to be a source of friction among some Muslim community institutions that host public events asking whether 'Singing = Sinning?'[25] or circulate critical interviews with prominent Anglophone acapella rappers such as Napoleon or Muslim Belal.[26] This restrictivist perspective extends to other forms of Muslim cultural production such as the creation of material artefacts, with even committed Muslims expressing dismay at the prohibitive rulings of some religious scholars. The acclaimed Indonesian artist Abdul Djalil Pirous, for instance, lamented:

> The religious leaders and *'ulama* ... here never talk about art and culture. They are blind to art. They don't know what is meant by modern art. And they don't recognise it as a form of knowledge or its relationship to Islam. They don't know anything about that.[27]

Other devout Muslims, who rely on more pragmatic scholarship, have adopted the 'civilisational view' of authorities such as the Egyptian scholars Yusuf al-Qaradawi and Muhammad al-Ghazali, whose juristic positions argued that religious reform of Muslim societies needs to integrate Islamic values with dominant cultural domains such as music, television, cinema and literature. This accommodationist view finds that conscious faith-based artistic expressions, or what has been called 'purposeful art' or 'art with a mission', to be conditionally permissible and justified on the basis of the intention to diffuse Islamic values and provide alternatives to counter the influence of European and American materialistic consumerism and popular culture.[28]

The Emergence of British Muslim Cultural Creatives

In the UK, theoretical and terminology debates as to what constitutes Islamic or Islamicate art are less relevant than the perceived religious lawfulness of art forms. These intra-religious legal contestations range from the more flexible accommodationist perspective that appears to be increasingly dominant, allowing a flourishing artistic culture to emerge despite the opposition of critics. British Muslims are, in general, less affluent than their coreligionists on the other side of the Atlantic. Muslim institutions in the UK were developed in the second half of the twentieth century by poor, predominantly South Asian migrant workers who relied upon them for community and social security. Many mosques and educational institutions, as a result, became somewhat insular, maintaining strong ethno-cultural affiliations and strict gender norms. The last 30 years have witnessed a pushback against this from successive younger generations, who have gradually made limited headway into the mainstream, created their own spaces and, to some extent, effected change in the Muslim institutional landscape.[29] The emergence and efflorescence of British Muslim art have been part of this process, with independent artistic spaces providing space for women and other minoritised communities, while facilitating debates on taboo social and political subjects that can be difficult to discuss in many community networks and institutions.

The UK also has a distinctive scheme of equality, representation and multiculturalism and this framework, along with these sociological changes, has afforded Muslims greater presence in public institutions and protection by laws and policies.[30] Muslim identity has been given greater recognition as Muslims, especially those born in Britain, have entered higher professions – such as business, education, law and medicine – in greater numbers. Despite this, however, Muslims have a troubled relationship with the British heritage and museum sectors, which have been slow to admit the contributions of citizens from minority communities. British Muslim artists of all kinds battle not only against more conservative interpretations of Islam that emphasise piety over aesthetic production, but also a sector within which it is hard to find space let alone be supported financially.

Neither of these two barriers has stopped Muslim youth from moving forward and making spaces for their voices to be heard. As Hussein Kesvani observes in his book *Follow Me Akhi: The Online World of British Muslims*, young Muslim Britons are digital natives who use the Internet and social media to determine their religious identities and cultures on their own terms.[31] This has led to evolving shifts in their understanding of their faith and the cultural production that has arisen from it. This confirms similar conclusions made by Gary Bunt in his recent book *Hashtag Islam: How Cyber-Islamic Environments Are Transforming Religious Authority*, by profiling self-styled preachers, YouTube influencers and dating apps that are significant shapers of various Muslim youth subcultures and redefining what it means to be British Muslims in the early twenty-first century.[32] This new wave of Millennials and Zoomers have reconfigured various boundaries of and reoriented the direction of and performance of Muslim arts, music, media and fashion tastes. Among the many emerging online platforms that promote British Muslim arts is the Khidr Collective – a multidisciplinary arts platform that curates and promotes the work of writers, poets, illustrators, filmmakers and photographers through its biannual publication and social media presence.[33] Another notable example of this expanding space is Bayt al-Fann ('House of Art' in Arabic), a British Muslim-led social media initiative that showcases art and culture, architecture and history with the intention of co-creating the future arts inspired by Islamic tradition.[34]

Social media has become one of the cutting-edge sites of creativity, particularly YouTube, which is an incubator for influencer culture, podcasts, commentators, vloggers, pranksters, tutorialists and religious authorities to global audiences. Critical voices have questioned the rise of Muslim social media influencers and accused them of becoming enmeshed in a shallow narcissistic, celebrity culture and consumerism that condones behaviours at odds with Islamic values.[35] While some of these Muslim content producers have produced innovative artistic synthesis, conservative religious voices have questioned the religious lawfulness of their output, language and use of hyphenated self-descriptors, arguing instead for a 'culture free Islam' that allows Muslims to see themselves just as people who happen to be living in Britain. The idea of a 'British Islam' remains controversial in large part because great emphasis has been placed on the notion by successive governments as part of counterextremism policies; critics consequently see its 'effective function [as being] to discipline a minority whose religion will never be allowed to fully fit in'.[36] Yet despite this internal resistance and political sensitivity, for many Muslims an encultured 'Islam of the British Isles', with its different flavours of English, Scottish, Irish and Welsh Muslimness, continues to be appealing and consider it as an identity worth creating. It should also be pointed out that are no 'monolithic understandings of

Muslimness' and the term 'British Muslim' as 'a concept/identity is not singular nor static, but exponential and vehicular – it is always contingent and contested, multiple and in motion'.[37] The contestation of such identities parallels the notion of a 'European Islam', an ongoing project of Muslim cultural indigenisation that has been a work in process for decades and predates the securitised policy discourses following 9/11 and 7/11 terrorist attacks.[38] In the case of the UK, various activist and artistic projects have been claiming a distinct British Muslim identity since the early 1990s, and effectively recovering older iterations of an anglicised Islamic culture.[39] One such case is *Everyday Muslim*, an online oral history project lead by Sadiya Ahmed, which seeks to create a centralised archive of experiences of individuals and communities documenting unmediated portrayals of British Muslim life. On the other end of the spectrum are writers, actors and storytellers who are shaping a contemporary Britannic Crescent.

Whilst some Muslim artists – notably the actor and rapper Riz Ahmed, who in 2020 became the first Muslim to be nominated for the Best Actor Oscar – have made huge progress in their respective fields, many others have struggled for recognition. Most find it difficult to present their work in mainstream establishments such as theatres, galleries and museums – places which, as this volume shows, regularly include objects from the 'Muslim world', but offer little acknowledgement of the work of contemporary Muslim artists (see Chapters 2, 7 and 8 in this volume). Many upcoming Muslim artists work alone, struggle to fund their projects and often encounter substantial challenges in trying to network with mainstream practitioners to advise them on how to grow, fund and sustain their areas of work. This state of affairs is increasingly challenged and a few artists are managing to get exposure for their work. One example is Aisha Zia, a playwright behind an exhibition showcasing British Muslim artists, who explained, 'I want to change the narrative that is presented to us. There is lots of negative portrayal about communities. It's about offering an alternative so people [...] feel less isolated'.[40] Another two other artists who succeeded in displaying their work are Faisal Hussain, who creates provocative pieces that 'question perceptions, undermine racist, anti-Muslim stereotypes and highlights missing histories and overlooked facts'. His 'Suspect Suspects, Suspect Objects' exhibition comprised objects designed to lampoon the absurdity of Islamophobia and state securitisation in Britain: 'Muzlamic Ray Guns', 'Prevent Cup Cakes' and 'Michael Gove's Trojan Horse'.[41] Similarly, Alaa Alsaraji's artistry explores the issues such as identity, faith and race in her *Mapping Sanctuaries* interactive exhibition – a collection of digital illustrations and sound pieces exploring 'notions of safety and the spaces that exist between isolation and belonging within Muslim communities'.[42]

Over the last two decades, the Khayaal Theatre Company has developed a pioneering reputation for delivering stagecraft inspired by Muslim heritages and cultures and has produced several cross-cultural productions that impart wisdom and humour. Among a newer generation of actors and performers, a small number have been able to break into the mainstream after building up their profiles on social media and comedy circuit such as Ali Shahalom and Aatif Nawaz. The pair worked together to develop the BBC 3 sketch show 'Muzlamic', which satirises modern Muslim life and social issues such as white fragility, racial stereotyping and unconscious biases.[43] Another kindred soul is Nabil Abdulrashid, a British Nigerian comic, who is part of a small cluster of Muslim comics that sharpened their trade over the last decade in tours such as *Don't Panic, and I'm Islamic* and have now found success for his memorable appearances on Britain's Got Talent. However, that popularity came at a personal cost as Abdulrashid was subjected to death threats and the broadcast regulator OFCOM received thousands of complaints about his performances.[44] This public reaction uncomfortably highlights the polarised social climate of modern Britain. More recently, the phenomenon of anti-Black prejudice within Muslim communities has also been exposed and challenged by British Muslims of African and Caribbean heritage, who argue that they are not represented and respected within the homogenised perception of Islam in Britain.[45] This has generated in an increasing number of events exploring Black Muslim identity and heritage in the UK. A major instance of this counter-narrative was the 2020 online 'Black Muslim Renaissance Festival'. organised by the writer Na'ima Robert.[46] These types of intra-Muslim friction further highlight the contested nature of cultural identity construction in Muslim minority contexts like Britain.

In other domains, many gifted new authors have been literally 'rewriting the narrative' through works of fiction, memoirs, novellas and biographies, with the most popular produced by women. This ranges from so-called 'Muslim chick lit' stories to reflections in anthologies such as *It's Not about the Burqa: Muslim Women on Faith, Feminism, Sexuality and Race*, unfiltered musings on relationships in *Match Made in Heaven: British Muslim Women Write about Love and Desire*, to gripping topical novels like *Just Another Jihadi Jane* – a fictionalised account of two teenagers in northern England that become radicalised and join ISIS in Syria. This surge of cultural creatives enables the celebration and general public inclusion of talent in platforms, such as the Muslim Arts and Culture Festival, founded by the novelist Qaisra Shahraz, which is hosted across the North West annually. This is in addition to the various other literary events and Muslim Lifestyle Expos that are appearing across the country.[47] The appointment of Hanan Issa, a Welsh-Iraqi poet, film maker as the fifth national poet of Wales also gestures to this mainstreaming.

This women-led trend is explored in detail in a new book on *British Muslim Women in the Cultural and Creative Industries*, and complements the themes discussed in this collection.[48] With one or two notable exceptions, the developments described above are not well-known. Even in the voluminous academic literature on Islamic Britain, the artistic lives of British Muslims have been given limited coverage, meaning the role played by Muslim artists in reshaping British Islam is hardly recognised.[49] In both academic and popular presses, Muslims are limited to being aggressors or victims, with strategies of creative resistance generally being ignored.[50]

The Features of this Volume

This volume seeks to address some of these limitations through a collaboration between scholars and Muslim artists, curators and arts sector practitioners. It includes analysis of Muslim art as a category and a movement, as well as accounts of people working in theatre, popular music, the heritage sector and ancient and modern visual arts. It shows how Muslim arts have grown in part due to changes in British Muslim communities, looks at the difficulties they face and considers steps to facilitate more Muslim artists entering the mainstream. The volume developed out of a conference organised by the Muslims in Britain Research Network (MBRN) in September 2017. MBRN is an organisation that, especially since 2014, has consciously sought to bridge the gaps between academia and Muslim communities, and this event gathered academics, artists, researchers and members of the public to address the theme of British Muslim cultural production and how it relates the exploration of questions of identity, belonging and social change. Panels critically discussed various topics such as what does contemporary 'Muslim' and 'Islamic' art mean, how are Muslim arts in Britain developing and if the cultural industries are responding to the emergence of British Muslim artists. These questions also reflect conversations taking place within Muslim communities around the nature of artist expression and the difficulties in gaining recognition and funding outside of the mainstream and uneasy tensions within communities as about certain forms of visual and performance.

The purpose of the collection is to profile emerging forms of British Muslim art and, through doing this, prompt a debate about its value and inclusion in UK society. As a collaboration between scholars and practitioners, this anthology includes scholarly contributions as well as reflective accounts of artists' own practice and experience of working at the margins of the British Arts sector. The authors we have included in this volume approach their subject matter from very different starting positions. Some offer descriptive sociological accounts of British Muslim art as a movement, other essays describe personal experiences of being marginalised in the arts sector, while others outline a theology of Islamic art. Our hope is that the contrast between the chapters allows readers to see more vividly the different perspectives rather than simply describing them abstractly.

The collection is structured around three sections that deal, respectively, with: I) the cultural politics of British Muslim artistic production; II) art in contemporary British Muslim culture; and III) the inclusion (and marginalisation) of British Muslim art in the wider UK arts sector. Section I seeks to set the scene with two contributions that outline the agendas of animating Muslim art and the challenges facing it. In Chapter 1, Carl Morris, an academic specialising in British Muslim cultural production, elucidates the category of 'British Muslim art' by comparing it to two other arts movements that emerged in the United States in the 1970s: the Black Arts Movement (BAM) and Contemporary Christian Music (CCM). The former of these sought to shape black consciousness and resistance, preaching a message of self-reliance in the face of a hostile society but ultimately impacting upon American popular culture at large. The latter sought to create an alternative to secular pop, mimicking its themes but fusing it with a Christian message at odds with the mainstream American popular culture. Both of these movements, Morris suggests, are reflected in the category of British Muslim art. Muslim artists, marginalised by the mainstream, have typically sought to generate an independent cultural economy in a hostile society and many include social and political critiques as part of their work. Yet at the same time, much British Muslim cultural products, especially in the nasheed industry and other forms of music, shares themes with CCM. Looking at the fates of these two movements, Morris argues, offers lessons for understanding the nature and possible futures of British Muslim art: one involving the production of 'halal' alternatives to secular culture, and another developing along political lines and potentially reshaping the mainstream by challenging British society directly.

In Chapter 2, Shaheen Kasmani, a freelance artist, curator and producer, offers a personal reading of a theme that is developed across many of the later chapters – that of how Muslim artists relate to and oppose the 'colonial gaze' in the arts sector. Decolonisation has become a prominent theme across the arts, culture and heritage sectors as well as in higher education. Initially associated with the 'Rhodes Must Fall' movement that emerged in South Africa in the mid-2010s, the concept has spread across continents and now acts as a rallying cry in many debates about diversity and representation in the UK as well as further afield. Indeed, there is a small but important and growing literature about decolonising the arts.[51] Kasmani contends that decolonisation is a potentially powerful idea involving a confrontation with the legacy of colonialism and White supremacy that doesn't hide behind the tokenistic and repetitive conversations around diversity. She also draws attention to aspects of Eurocentrism, colonialism and racialisation that have been neglected in debates about decolonisation. Kasmani suggests that the transfer of Islamic art into élite museum contexts that are oriented around colonial logics routinely involves the secularisation of Islamic art: collections of objects that come under the heading of 'Islamic', 'Asian' and 'African' art are celebrated, conserved and lauded for the technical skill involved in their making, but the specifically religious themes and inner meanings are eroded. She also provides examples of how museums and the wider arts and culture sector overlook the historical and contemporary contributions of Muslim women and black Muslims. By offering an account of what her art means to her, Kasmani highlights how the colonial gaze erases meaning and value. The decolonisation of Islamic art, Kasmani thus concludes, must involve not only a confrontation with questions of race but with religious themes too.

Section II develops on these chapters by exploring how art is impacting and reshaping British Muslim communities, as well as British popular culture. This section explores how second- and third-generation British Muslims, as part of a broader generational shift, have re-shaped a variety of musical and artistic styles. In Chapter 3, Bradford-based artist Razwan ul-Haq outlines his distinctive style of calligraphy, which fuses traditional practices with graffiti and comic book art. Although to the outside observer, ul-Haq's images may seem modern and even insouciant in style, he explains how all his work is underpinned by a philosophy of 'Islamic minimalism' that has historical and theological roots. His art is, he explains, based on the concept of *fitra*, meaning 'natural balance'. Developing a personal argument rooted in his own experiences of travelling to Mecca, ul-Haq proposes that one can find parallels between the contemplative minimalism of traditional Persian Nastaliq calligraphy, on which he bases his art, and contemplations of the 'signs' of God in nature, such as a stream of water, a flame or trembling leaves. Through this connection with the concept of fitra, calligraphic art provides the artist with a certain disposition in which two Islamic ethical concepts are central: first, that of *husn*, meaning the good or the beautiful; and second, that of *zuhd*, meaning contemplative detachment. Nastaliq calligraphy can be regarded as 'Islamic', then, in its alignment with Islamic cosmology and ethical principles.

In Chapter 4, Ayesha Khan examines how the interaction between transnational Sufism and the sociological environment in Britain has led to new forms of Sufi expression, including creative and syncretism artistic forms. The chapter focuses on recitation of Sufi *naat khwaani* – mystical poetry, which was popular amongst first- and second-generation South Asian British Barelvi Muslims and performed in *mehfils* within private homes and religious institutions. Khan shows how *naat khwaani* has become widespread amongst viewers of British Muslim TV shows popularised, especially among British Muslim youth, through social media videos on YouTube and Facebook live, and how this popularisation has led to a fierce debate about its status as a religious practice. Khan illustrates how, as Sufi traditions transfer across different contexts and localities, there is a struggle among many Muslims to pass down a tradition to subsequent generations. In the earlier periods, Sufism in Britain was mostly practiced within specific communities and propagated by migrants from the Muslim world. These migrants maintained the Sufi traditions of their places of origin, including their association with Sufi *tariqa*s. However, today young British Muslims are exploring Sufism in new and innovative ways. Research on contemporary Sufism has shown how traditional modes of *tariqa* are now changing to adapt to a modern global context, with distinctive styles of Sufism emerging and giving rise to multitariqa Sufi conferences, post-tariqa Sufi movements and individual articulations of Sufi identity.

In Chapter 5, Abdul-Azim Ahmed, a researcher specialising in Muslim Britain, highlights the way Grime, a distinctively British offshoot of hip-hop, draws upon Islamic themes and fuses these with other religious references. The relationship between religion and hip-hop has been explored by numerous scholars, particularly those based in the United States, revealing a complex history intertwining the contours of Black music, Christianity and Islam. Grime, however, has received comparatively little attention. In his chapter, Ahmed considers what Grime and British hip-hop's references to Islamic themes can tell us about contemporary religion. He argues that there is a religious literacy in Grime music that cuts against narratives of secularisation, indicating that, for some young British people, religion is a vibrant part of everyday life. Furthermore, he shows how the particular role of Muslim Grime artists, and the familiarity non-Muslim Grime artists have with Islam, reveals dynamic ways in which Islam has become embedded within British urban culture. This, he suggests, points towards a form of religious literacy embedded in everyday multiculture, one that sits at odds with most contemporary advocates for the promotion of religious literacy, whose writings tend to be justified either in terms of liberal citizenship education or conservative emphasis upon the value of learning established national traditions.

Finally, Section III turns to look at the experiences of Muslim artists who work in the theatre, museum and the performing arts sectors. In Chapter 6, Hassan Mahamdallie, a playwright and the founder of the theatre company Dervish Productions, focuses on the question of whether

theatre can be counted as one of the few spaces in Britain where artists –
and British Muslim artists specifically – can discuss political themes in
an imaginative way that challenges public preconceptions and dogmas.
He contrasts the experience of his own independently produced play on
British Somali experience, *The Crows Plucked Your Sinews*, with that of
Homegrown, a play about youth radicalisation written by Omar El-Khairy
and directed by Nadia Latif for the National Youth Theatre (NYT).
Homegrown was abruptly cancelled by the NYT management towards the
end of rehearsals and following meetings with Camden Police. Exploring
the reasons behind the play's cancellation, Mahamdallie argues that while
mainstream theatre often professes a willingness to tell stories that are 'on
the edge' and divide opinion, this rarely extends to allowing Muslims to
explore issues from their viewpoints and experiences. This, he suggests, is
one reason why theatre – like most other creative industries – is dominated
by people from upper-middle-class origins, with working-class people and
those from an ethnic and religious minority background increasingly excluded. Although those working and participating in the creative industries are generally more 'liberal' in outlook than other elements of British
society, Mahamdallie contends that this cultural class is, ultimately, a
closed network and that only grassroots theatre has the capacity to
facilitate fundamental social change.

In Chapter 7, Neelam Hussain, the curator of the Mingana Collection
of Middle Eastern Manuscripts at the University of Birmingham, discusses the challenges and opportunities of using heritage material to
engage with Muslim communities, schools and the wider public and
points to lessons that can be learned from the successes and failures of
her and her colleagues' engagement efforts. Containing over 2000 Arabic
and Persian manuscripts, the Mingana Collection of Middle Eastern
Manuscripts ranges from religious, scientific, literary and poetic texts
that include miniature paintings and examples of the decorative book
arts. The collection provides a unique and rich source of material both
for academic research and exploration of Islamic intellectual, literary
and artistic heritage. The Cadbury Research Library has delivered various public engagement projects linked to the Mingana Collection, the
most significant of these being an exhibition of one of the earliest surviving manuscripts of Qur'an in the world. This manuscript – often referred to as the 'Birmingham Qur'an' – has often been portrayed as an
emblem for the city of Birmingham and a reflection of the fact that it has
the largest Muslim population in the UK outside of London. At the
same time, the prominence of this and other projects, Hussain contends,
cannot hide the fact that museums and other élite institutions face
institutional and cultural challenges that need to be addressed for
projects to be meaningful to local communities, including comparatively
deprived Muslim communities.

In Chapter 8, Sara Choudhrey, a scholar and artist who applies digital techniques to traditional pattern making, draws on her own experiences as well as interviews with Muslim artists to offer an account of the significant difficulties that practitioners of Islamic art face. Using her research, she provides accounts of instances where curators have sought to avoid using the term 'Islam' in describing art collections and exhibitions, preferring instead to include Muslim artists in collections on the 'Middle East'. Reiterating and empirically reinforcing Kasmani's earlier chapter, she highlights how such acts of exclusion can lead to difficulties for practitioners of modern Islamic art whose work does not fit this frame and, moreover, is created in an environment of suspicion of Islam. As an artist, reaching the desired audience and maintaining one's creative vision is difficult regardless of who one is and where one comes from. Yet while all artists face considerable challenges developing a profile for their work and securing the income and space necessary to pursue their creative practice, these, Choudhrey argues, are amplified for artists from black and minority ethnic backgrounds who are underrepresented in the arts and have less access to opportunities when compared to their white–British counterparts. Add to this the problems arising from when artists seek to produce work that speaks to and about a specific group (Muslims) or tradition (Islam), and exclusions are compounded further, with artists being alienated from a sector that described them in deeply flawed terms.

This volume brings these threads together and explores the possible futures of British Muslim arts. We make the case that British Muslim art can be described not just by referring to its distinguishing characteristics but also in terms of *cultural change*. The emergence and development of British Muslim art can be seen as one chapter in a story about the embedding of Muslims and Islam in Britain, a story that sees both Islamic traditions and British society being re-shaped. As the preceding chapters amply demonstrate, this is a challenging story involving misrecognition discrimination, self-organisation and resistance. Progress is often slow or stop-start: the institutional responses across different sectors after the Black Lives marches in the summer of 2020 – in the form of reviews and reports – have yet to lead to meaningful change.[52] It is, however, also a story with positive and hopeful elements. British Muslims are increasingly embedded in British society and, as British-born Muslims move into middle age, finding routes into elite professions. This includes the arts, where an established cohort of Muslim professionals is beginning to find limited space and influence in mainstream institutions – setting up projects such as Arts Council England's 'Arts and Islam' initiative. Drawing from these instances, we map out a possible future for Muslim art, not just as an innovative presence within the wider British arts scene but also as a creative force that has the potential to unsettle established historical narratives of Islam's place in Europe.

Notes

1 Tim Adams. 'Art Gets Things in the Open' – British Muslim Artists Tell Their Stories. *The Guardian*, 12 April, 2015: https://www.theguardian.com/culture/2015/apr/12/young-british-muslim-artists-mohammed-ali-aveas-mohammad-yusra-warsama-aisha-zia [accessed 21 July 2022].
2 Harriet Sherwood. 'Meet Generation M: The Young, Affluent Muslims Changing the World'. *The Guardian*, 16 September 2016: https://www.theguardian.com/world/2016/sep/03/meet-generation-m-the-young-affluent-muslims-changing-the-world [accessed 21 July 2022]. See also Shelina Janmohamed. *Generation M: Young Muslims Changing the World*. London: I.B.Tauris, 2016.
3 Aina Khan. 'Black Female Muslim Emcees'. *Vogue Arabia*, October 2020: https://en.vogue.me/culture/black-female-muslim-emcees/ [accessed 21 July 2022].
4 Aina Khan. 'Black Female Muslim Emcees'. *Vogue Arabia*, October 2020: https://en.vogue.me/culture/black-female-muslim-emcees/ [accessed 21 July 2022]. For more on contemporary Black Muslim Hip-hop cultures see Su'ad Abdul Khabeer. *Muslim Cool: Race, Religion, and Hip Hop in the United States*. New York: NYU Press, 2016.
5 Ginia Bellafante. 'Islam, Hope and Charity Inspire Dealer Turned Rapper'. Television review: 'The New Muslim Cool'. *Ney York Times*, 22 June 2009: http://www.nytimes.com/2009/06/23/arts/television/23view.html?_r=0 [accessed 21 July 2022]. This can also be seen in the work of other American Muslim converts who have returned to the pre-Islamic cultural roots and reconciled their Muslim and non-Muslim aspects of their identity, for example see Mustafa Davis. *Deen Tight: A Documentary Film*. Mustafa Davis Studios, 2011. Available online at: https://vimeo.com/27049587 [accessed 21 July 2022].
6 Hisham Aidi. *Rebel Music: Race, Empire and the New Muslim Youth Culture*. New York: Vintage, 2014.
7 Daniel DeHanas, Renasha Khan, and Peter Mandaville. *Living the Muslim Atlantic: Race, Gender, and the Politics of Marginality*. London: King's College London, 2020: https://www.britishcouncil.us/sites/default/files/living_the_muslim_atlantic.pdf [accessed 21 July 2022]. These transatlantic associations between Islam, music and political activism are also explored in Suhail Daulatzai's, *Black Star, Crescent Moon*, where here details the shared history of Black Muslims, radical activists, and the Muslim World, who forged global connections and political alliances which led to vibrant exchange of musical influences in different Muslim communities in the USA, Europe and Latin America.
8 Malcolm X remains a perennially fascinating figure for people around the world; a newer generation were introduced to his life and legacy through the gripping Netflix documentary Who Killed Malcolm X? in 2020. See Ark Media, *Who Killed Malcom X?* 2020: https://www.netflix.com/gb/title/80217478 [accessed 22 July 2022]. For more on Malcom X's cultural and artistic impact on contemporary British and American Muslims see Yolanda van Tilborgh. 'Expressions of Political Theology in Art and Islam: Malcolm

X-Inspired Transformations among Muslims in the US and the UK'. *Svensk Teologisk Kvartalskrift,* 96 (1), 2020, pp. 61–68.

9 A useful introduction to Islamic art historical scholarship is provided in Hannah Lise Simonson. 'What does Islamic Art Mean for Islam? An Examination of Word/Image in the Calligraphic works of Nja Mahdaoui, Mohamed Zakariya, and Kamal Boullata'. PhD thesis. Reed College, Portland, OR, 2011; and Wendy M. K. Shaw. *What is 'Islamic' Art? Between Religion and Perception.* Cambridge: Cambridge University Press, 2019.

10 For more on the contested nature of the subject see Judith Ernst. 'The Problem of Islamic Art'. In Miriam Cooke and Bruce B. Lawrence, *Muslim Networks: From Hajj to Hip-Hop.* Chapel Hill, NC: University of North Carolina Press, 2006, pp. 107–131.

11 Wendy M. K. Shaw. 'The Islam in Islamic Art History: Secularism and Public Discourse'. *Journal of Art Historiography* 6 (June 1, 2012): 1–34; Wendy M. K. Shaw. *What Is "Islamic" Art? Between Religion and Perception.* Cambridge, United Kingdom: Cambridge University Press, 2019. Notably, however, such scholarship does often suggest that Islamic art begins with the Prophet Muhammad. See Avinoam Shalem. 'What Do We Mean When We Say "Islamic Art"? A Plea for a Critical Rewriting of the History of the Arts of Islam'. *Journal of Art Historiography,* no. 6 (June 2012): 6.

12 Oludamini Ogunnaike, Aishah Holland, and Ian Whiteman. 'What Makes Art Islamic?' Interview at 'The Silent Theology of Islamic Art, Zaytuna College, Berkley, CA, 17 December 2017: https://www.youtube.com/watch? v=qi3jyhYORRc&ab_channel=Renovatio%3ATheJournalofZaytunaCollege [accessed 22 July 2022].

13 Umar F. Abdullah. *Innovation and Creativity in Islam.* Chicago: An Nawawi Foundation. 2006, p. 1. Citing Noah Feldman. *After Jihad: America and the Struggle for Islamic Democracy.* New York: Farrar, Straus and Giroux, 2003, pp. 11–12.

14 Marshall G. Hodgson. *Venture of Islam.* Chicago: Chicago University Press, 1974, p. 59.

15 The phrase 'Arts of the Islamic World' also acknowledges that not all of the work produced in the Islamic world was for Muslims or created by Muslims. Islamic art is not a monolithic style or movement; it spans 1,300 years of history. The Islamic arts incorporated the techniques and methods of Roman, West African, Byzantine, Sassanid, Central Asian, and Chinese artists to give birth to a new art depicting the new religion's vision of reality.

16 There is a large body of literature that spans Islamic influence of Western art forms for more than a thousand years. See for example Rosamond E. Mack. *Bazaar to Piazza: Islamic Trade and Italian Art, 1300–1600.* Oakland, CA: University of California Press, 2001.

17 Oludamini Ogunnaike. 'The Silent Theology of Islamic Art'. *Renvatio: The Journal of Zaytuna College,* 5 December 2017: https://renovatio.zaytuna.edu/ article/the-silent-theology-of-islamic-art [accessed 22 July 2022].

18 Seyyed Hossein Nasr. *Islamic Art and Spirituality.* Albany, NY: SUNY Press, 1994.

19 Pierre Bourdieu. *The Rules of Art: Genesis and Structure of the Literary Field.* Stanford, CA: Stanford University Press. 1996.

20 Richard Bulliet. *Islam: The View from the Edge.* New York, NY: Columbia University Press, 1994, p. 195.

21 Yolanda van Tilborgh. 'Conversion Strategies and the Power to Define: British and American Muslim Performance in Bourdieu's Field of Art'. *Sociology and Anthropology*, 4(5), 2016, pp. 320–330.
22 Nasr Abu Zay. 'The Modernization of Islam or the Islamization of Modernity'. In Roel Meijer (ed.) *Cosmopolitanism, Identity and Authenticity in the Middle East*. Curzon Press, 1999, pp. 71–86.
23 Susan Babie. 'Voices of Authority: Locating the "Modern" in "Islamic" Arts'. *Getty Research Journal*, 3, 2011, pp. 135–51.
24 See for example, The Irish Times. 'Scholars and Musicians Hotly Debate whether Music is Permissible or Not'. *The Irish Times*, 21 July, 2006: https://www.irishtimes.com/news/scholars-and-musicians-hotly-debate-whether-music-is-permissible-or-not-1.1262467 [accessed 22 July 2022].
25 'Music—Singing or Sinning?', organised by Salafi-oriented performance poet Lori Zakariya King, was part of the 'Express Yourself' conference held in the London Muslim Centre, East London Mosque, 2009. Cited in Yolanda van Tilborgh, 'Islam, Culture and Authoritative Voices in the UK and the US: Patterns of Orientation and Autonomy among Muslims in Art'. *Zeitschrift für Religion, Gesellschaft und Politik*, 2, pp. 101–134.
26 Roadside2Islam. 'The Fitnah of Music: Muslim Belal, Maskiah and UK Apache'. *YouTube*: https://www.youtube.com/watch?v=v0ycVwrfgk4 [accessed 22 July 2022].
27 Kenneth M George. *Picturing Islam: Art and Ethics in a Muslim Lifeworld*. Chichester: Wiley-Blackwell, 2010, p. 4
28 Yolanda van Tilborgh, 'Islam, Culture and Authoritative Voices in the UK and the US: Patterns of Orientation and Autonomy among Muslims in Art'. *Zeitschrift für Religion, Gesellschaft und Politik*, 2, pp. 101–134.
29 Stephen H Jones. *Islam and the Liberal State: National Identity and the Future of Muslim Britain*. London: Bloomsbury/IB Tauris, 2021.
30 Nasar Meer. *Citizenship, Identity and the Politics of Multiculturalism: The Rise of Muslim Consciousness*. Basingstoke: Palgrave Macmillan, 2010.
31 Hussein Kesvani, *Follow Me, Akhi: The Online World of British Muslims*. London: Hurst, 2019.
32 Gary R. Bunt. *Hashtag Islam: How Cyber-Islamic Environments Are Transforming Religious Authority*. Chapel Hill, NC: University of North Carolina Press, 2018.
33 For more information, see: https://khidrcollective.co.uk
34 For more information, see: https://bayatalfann.com
35 For example, Amarah Fahimuddin. 'Muslim Sensationalism Sells'. *The Muslimah Diaries*, 12 May 2017: https://themuslimahdiaries.com/2017/05/12/muslim-youtubers-sensationalism-sells/comment-page-1/ [accessed 18 May 2019].
36 This is explored further in Stephen H. Jones. *Islam and Liberal State*. London: I.B. Tauris, 2020, p.4. Despite these reservations, it is worth noting that the creation of a coherent organic British Muslimness was attempted over a 100 years ago through the efforts of prominent English converts such as the 'Shaykh of the British Isles' Abdullah Quilliam, Lady Evelyn Cobbold and Marmaduke Pickthall. For further information see: Jamie Gilham. *Loyal Enemies: British Converts to Islam, 1850–1950*. London, Hurst, 2014.
37 Carl Morris. 'Re-Placing the Term "British Muslim": Discourse, Difference and the Frontiers of Muslim Agency in Britain'. *Journal of Muslim Minority Affairs*, 38 (3), 2018, pp. 409–427.

38 See for example Jorgen Nielsen. *Towards a European Islam*. Palgrave Macmillan, 1999.

39 More background can be found in Sadek Hamid. *Sufis Salafis Islamists: The Contested Ground of British Islamic Activism*. I.B. Tauris, 2017.

40 BBC News. 'British Muslim Artists Showcased in New Peterborough Gallery'. *BBC*, 3 April 2019: https://www.bbc.co.uk/news/uk-england-cambridgeshire-47734574 [accessed 22 July 2022].

41 Each of these three exhibits alludes to a high-profile episode of Muslim securitisation (the UK government's Prevent programme, the so-called "Trojan Horse" affair in Birmingham) or Islamophobia (a far-right English Defence League supporter complaining of "Muslamic Ray Guns"). Hussain's exhibit was on display at the Brunei Gallery, SOAS between 12 January and 21 March 2021.

42 It can be visited online at: https://www.mappingsanctuaries.co.uk

43 See Adnan Ahmed. 'Muzlamic'. *BBC Three*, 2019: https://www.bbc.co.uk/programmes/p07g0j3p [accessed 22 July 2022].

44 Lanre Bakare. 'Comedian Nabil Abdulrashid Received Death Threats after Routines about Race'. *The Guardian*, 2 November 2020: https://www.theguardian.com/tv-and-radio/2020/nov/02/britains-got-talent-comedian-nabil-abdulrashid-death-threats-race [accessed 22 July 2022].

45 See for example Momtaza Mehri. 'Black, British & Muslim: We're not just a "Complication"'. *Media Diversified*, 30 March 2015: https://mediadiversified.org/2015/03/30/black-british-muslim-were-not-just-a-complication/ [accessed 22 July 2022].

46 Na'ima B Robert. 'Black Muslims Are almost Invisible in Britain, But Now We're Carving Out a Space'. *The Guardian*, 10 October 2020: https://www.theguardian.com/commentisfree/2020/oct/10/black-muslims-invisible-britain-minority [accessed 22 July 2022].

47 For example, a major "Muslim Lifestyle Expo" is held every year in Manchester and glossy lifestyle brochures such as British Muslim Lifestyle, cash in on the appetite for faith-based goods and services.

48 Saskia Warren. *British Muslim Women in the Cultural and Creative Industries*. Edinburgh: Edinburgh University Press, 2022.

49 There are some notable exceptions, including: Anamik Saha, '"Beards, Scarves, Halal Meat, Terrorists, Forced Marriage": Television Industries and the Production of "Race"'. *Media, Culture & Society* 34 (4), 2012, pp.424–38; Philip Lewis and Sadek Hamid. *British Muslims: New Directions in Islamic Thought, Creativity and Activism*. Edinburgh: Edinburgh University Press, 2018; Carl Morris. '"Look into the Book of Life": Muslim Musicians, Sufism and Postmodern Spirituality in Britain'. *Social Compass* 63 (3), 2016, pp. 389–404.

50 Again, with some exceptions: Christina Pantazis and Simon Pemberton. 'Resisting the Advance of the Security State: The Impact of Frameworks of Resistance on the UK'S Securitisation Agenda'. *International Journal of Law, Crime and Justice* 41 (4), 2013, pp.358–74; Katherine E. Brown. 'Contesting the Securitisation of British Muslims: Citizenship and Resistance'. *Interventions* 12 (2), 2010, pp. 171–82.

51 See: Amy Lonetree. *Decolonizing Museums: Representing Native America in National and Tribal Museums*. Chapel Hill: University North Carolina Press, 2012. Claire Smith. 'Decolonising the Museum: The National Museum of the

American Indian in Washington, DC'. *Antiquity* 79, no. 304 (June 2005): 424–39. https://doi.org/10.1017/S0003598X00114206. For a discussion focusing on Islamic art see: Wendy M. K. Shaw. *What Is "Islamic" Art? Between Religion and Perception.* Cambridge, United Kingdom: Cambridge University Press, 2019.

52 Jade Montserrat, Cecilia Wee and Michelle Williams Gamaker. 'We Need Collectivity against Structural and Institutional Racism in the Cultural Sector'. *Arts Professional,* 24 June 2020: "We need collectivity against structural and institutional racism in the cultural sector" | ArtsProfessional [accessed 22 July 2022].

Part I

The Cultural Politics
of British Muslim
Artistic Production

1 A British Muslim Arts Movement

Public Politics or Religious Devotion?

Carl Morris

Introduction

In 1976, the Newark Congress of African People – one of the leading Black Power organisations in the United States – was evicted from its headquarters in New Jersey. Founded and headed by the controversial poet and activist, Amiri Baraka, this was the end of a radical and formative era. Shaped by discourses concerning African American self-reliance and self-determination, it was a period that brought together politics and art, providing a vital link that advanced Black consciousness from the agitation of figures such as Marcus Garvey and Malcolm X, through to the mainstream cultural and social success of African American writers, musicians and artists, from Toni Morrison through to Mos Def (aka Yasiin Bey).[1] In the same year, a world away from the hothouse politics of Newark, a 15-year-old Amy Grant performed her first song, Mountain Top, at Harpeth Hall School in Nashville. Combining gentle piano melodies, echoing the sound of 1970s pop music, with uplifting lyrics concerning Christian worship and praise, the song was initially recorded by her church youth leader before being picked up by a Christian record label, Word Records, for her debut album, *Amy Grant*. This was the beginning of a career that would see Amy Grant – known in subsequent decades as the 'Queen of Christian Pop' – rise to become a central figure in a wider American Christian entertainment culture.[2]

At this point, you might be wondering what Amiri Baraka and Amy Grant have got to do with one another and how on earth are they relevant for British Muslim art and culture in Britain. While not connected in any direct sense, I will argue in this chapter that the Black Arts Movement (BAM) and Contemporary Christian Music (CCM) throw important comparative light on our understanding of what has been called a 'British Muslim Arts Movement'. The term itself is not mine but is rather a label that has been used, a little cautiously and sometimes in an offhand way, by British Muslim artists in speculative conversations and internet debates

DOI: 10.4324/9781003330714-3

about the future of 'Muslim art' in Britain. It makes no sense for me to try to provide the term with meaning or to ask whether it is appropriate or not – after all, I am neither Muslim nor an artist. But as an academic working in the fields of religion, sociology and cultural studies, I can draw some comparative allusions that might help us think about the term. As I argue, the successes and difficulties of BAM and CCM highlight the opportunities and restrictions that exist when labelling any self-conscious arts movement, particularly one that is bound together so inextricably with issues of ethnicity and public religion.

It is an exciting time to think about British Muslim involvement in the arts – particularly if we expand our definition of the arts to include Muslim cultural production ranging from film and comedy through to performance and visual art. The examples are too numerous to list but range from feature films, such as *Freesia* and *Blessed are the Strangers*, through to comedians like Tez Ilyas and Sadia Azmat, to visual artists such as Mohammed Ali Aerosol, playwrights and theatres, such as the Khayaal Theatre Company, and to musicians like global superstar Sami Yusuf and pop-nasheed performer Saif Adam. These examples merely scratch the surface – it would take a book-length publication to even barely give all this cultural activity the attention it deserves.

While self-conscious British Muslim art and culture has been bubbling away for decades, it is perhaps only in recent years that a critical mass of resources, activity and confidence have started to come together. New networks and platforms are emerging to better create and share Muslim cultural activity. This is all interlinked, from the creative hubs of fashion and design, to street art, photography and community theatre, through to the launching of digital streaming services with international reach, such as Alchemiya and Ali Huda. It also has great potential – as well as significant challenges – in reaching out beyond Muslim audiences. While Muslims in Britain are still more often talked *about*, faint cracks are nonetheless starting to appear in mainstream culture, from the commissioning of original British Muslim content by the BBC, through to public events such as the Festival of Muslim Cultures and Ideas hosted by the British Library in April 2018.

But should this undoubted cultural innovation and activity be labelled? What does it mean for us to talk about a 'British Muslim Arts Movement'? BAM and CCM are useful in thinking about these questions. They have both been shaped by specific audiences – BAM was explicitly producing art for African Americans (and a wider Black diaspora) while CCM was similarly aimed at Christian believers in the United States (and internationally). The values, assumptions and experiences of these distinct audiences shaped the artistic output of these movements – movements that were always marked by powerful, if contested, ideologies and aims. Similarly, both were supported by the development of specific cultural institutions, ranging from the African American publishing houses and community theatres of BAM to the Christian record labels of CCM. They were therefore tied explicitly to unique subcultures and micro-economies. Ultimately, the BAM faded away as a clear and organised movement, but not without first leaving a legacy of African American culture and agency that continues to shape American society to this day. Conversely, while CCM is still going strong as a distinct genre and subculture – with successful artists and record labels that inspire and mobilise Christian communities – the impact of CCM on wider American culture has been relatively minimal.

Over the course of this chapter, I examine the varying fortunes and features of both the BAM and CCM. I examine in turn the cultural economies, aesthetics and political critiques of these artistic movements in an attempt to shine some comparative light on the following questions:

i To what extent might an independent cultural economy help or hinder British Muslim art and culture?

ii Does recognition of a British Muslim Arts Movement necessarily assume that there is such a thing as British Muslim art?

iii How might a British Muslim Arts Movement develop a distinctive social and political critique?

I do not claim to have the answer to these questions, but I do make the more modest suggestion that the way in which they are addressed by Muslim artists and practitioners will probably shape the future outcome of any British Muslim Arts Movement. This drives to the heart of whether Muslim art and culture is an act of public politics and cultural debate, or whether it is a form of religious devotion and mobilisation. Different artists will cleave towards one or the other, but it is difficult for any coherent arts movement to simultaneously straddle both. Of course, both are equally useful and valid objectives – but they emerge as a result of strategic choices rather than just intentions. By better understanding the BAM and CCM, the nature of these choices might become a little clearer.

Cultural Economies: Building an Alternative

The BAM was a wider outgrowth of the Black Arts Repertory Theatre/ School, founded in 1965 in Harlem by LeRoi Jones, known later as Amiri Baraka. The movement was inspired by the rallying call of Malcolm X, echoing an existing tradition of African American resistance, to 'separate' rather than 'integrate' – to seek a new and independent future beyond the control of White America – that which Maulana Karenga described, broadly, as self-determination, self-respect and self-defence.[3] In Black communities across the United States, this led to forms of local empowerment – by Black people, for Black people – that ranged from urban regeneration and education to political mobilisation and, of course, artistic expression. This was Black Nationalism in action, developing a nation within a nation, although exactly how far this drive for 'independence' should be taken was always hotly debated. The BAM approached this challenge with gusto, seeking to circumvent an exclusionary mainstream culture industry by developing independent groups and institutions that would provide a platform for Black artists and writers, catering explicitly (and almost exclusively) for a Black audience, without the need for 'white patronage'. This included for the most part a range of interconnected publishing houses, periodicals and theatres, often with a focus on poetry, which was easier and cheaper to publish than larger monographs. The economic basis for the BAM therefore helped shape the aesthetic of an emerging art form – a spoken word poetics that ultimately birthed hip hop culture – by providing it with a secure and self-contained foundation that enabled a whole new generation of Black artists to emerge. However, while these institutions continue to exist in some form their significance has waned. Alternative routes that are no longer restricted along racial lines (larger publishing houses, record companies, magazines, etc.) have enabled Black artists to reach a wider audience. It is a measure of the success (if not the intent) of the BAM – which arose during a time of exclusion for many African American artists – that it no longer makes sense to just talk about 'Black art for Black people'. African American artists have risen to the highest peaks of acclaim and have become central pillars within the wider American cultural economy.

CCM emerged at a similar time, bringing together the counter-culturalism of the 1960s with the spiritual radicalism of Duane Pederson's Jesus Movement in California. These early advocates were immersed in the cultural radicalism of the era, but were evangelical Christians, often with a belief in spiritual gifts (such as faith healing and speaking in tongues), and were consequently searching for meaning beyond the arid consumerism and over-sexualisation of mainstream popular culture. Thus was born 'Jesus Music' – later known as CCM – that fused together forms of popular music with an evangelical Christian message. Early forerunners included the 'father' of CCM, Larry Norman, who released the first complete album for this new genre, *Upon This Rock*, through Capitol Records in 1969. While initially released via mainstream secular record companies, it was during the 1970s, and then more quickly through the 1980s, that independent Christian record labels began to emerge. These new institutions – such as Word Records and Myrrh Records – were created to support this fledging genre and to release music that was both a form of alternative Christian entertainment and an act of evangelical ministry. This new industry helped create coherence in an otherwise disparate subculture by gathering together Christian musicians and by helping to create and sustain a community of believers/consumers. The model for this new industry was the replication of a wider music business – shot through with a charitable and evangelical Christian ethos – that organised alternative events (such as Christian music festivals) and gave form to related outputs (such as music magazine *CCM – Christian Community Music*). A whole new set of cultural institutions were therefore created from the ground up, providing a platform for Christian popular culture in America and nurturing a generation of musicians that might otherwise have struggled to find a place within the secular and materialistic framework of the wider music industry. The success of this genre is undoubted, and it is now a multi-billion dollar industry, but crossover appeal has been limited and CCM musicians remain largely confined to CCM audiences and music labels. So despite this success – and unlike the BAM – CCM has largely failed to break out of its own distinct subculture and cultural economy.

Art and Aesthetics: Breaking New Ground

The legendary jazz musician, John Coltrane, is heralded as the standard bearer for a new Black aesthetic that sought to develop itself beyond the confines and assumptions of Western art. While there has never been any settled agreement about what a Black aesthetic actually is,[4] many African American artists have followed the inclinations of Amiri Baraka in imagining and creating a lineage of art that stretches from Africa through to America and the Black diaspora. This was further often tied to a radical Black Leftist counterculture that was explicitly opposed to neo-colonialism and drew on Gramscian ideas of hegemony and superstructure – that is, opposing the cultural norms that are seemingly responsible for racial and economic oppression. This new Black aesthetic took many forms. It is most evident in the musical experimentation that marked jazz in particular – deviating from Western musical modes through improvisation and the use of African sound – and to a lesser extent R&B and blues, but it also took form through other means. Poetry and theatre, performed on street corners and at political rallies, developed cadences and rhythms that gradually morphed into hip hop and spoken word. There were attempts to replicate this in written form, with experimentation through typography and lineation, while visual artists developed distinctive pieces through the use of creative techniques such as appropriation, collage and screen printing. Language itself was a vital part of this aesthetic, celebrating, developing and playing around with an African American vernacular. Finally, there was the emergence of important themes that could be examined through art, from Black bodies and Black spaces through to spiritual immanence and the legacy of slavery. Ultimately, then the BAM paved the way for new forms of artistic expression that continue to thrive as a vibrant part of not just American but indeed global culture.

CCM did something very different, with a focus on providing a variation of mainstream culture rather than seeking to transcend it or provide a distinct alternative. From the outset, there was a desire to articulate evangelical Christianity through familiar forms of music rather than to develop new sounds through experimentation. Innovation has therefore been downplayed, with an emphasis instead on making Christianity accessible and relevant through the familiar modes and tropes of popular music. There is a logic to this approach. With a concern that young people are attracted to wider popular culture, one that is seemingly morally deficient, evangelical Christians have argued that they can provide an alternative – just as entertaining, but also wholesome and spiritually uplifting. This approach has correspondingly spawned Christian variations of popular music genres, from 'Christian pop' and 'Christian rock' through to 'Christian metal' and 'Christian hip hop'. Without judging the quality or originality of such music, it is possible to suggest that these sub-genres not only fail to offer something new and distinct for a wider audience but that they simultaneously carry with them markers of exclusion – 'Christian pop' inevitably becomes 'pop for Christians'. Without the cutting-edge originality of experimentation and new musical forms, there is perhaps less to attract a wider audience than has often been the case with art developed in a more groundbreaking form. If Christian music is an ersatz alternative, rather than something entirely new, then non-evangelical Christian audiences are unlikely to give it a second glance when they already consume the 'real thing'.

Political and Social Critique: Turning Towards the Centre

It is a notable irony that the BAM – which derived from an ideological belief in Black independence and separateness – has ultimately done so much to impact upon social and political norms beyond African American communities. Inspired by Malcolm X, the movement was not looking necessarily to change the attitudes of White Americans (in contrast to the civil rights claims of Martin Luther King) but was instead aiming to revolutionise the consciousness of Black Americans. Yet in looking inward, it nonetheless held up a mirror to American society, which was not just built upon a bedrock of racial animus but was also marred by inequalities relating to class and gender. The BAM managed to achieve this for several reasons. First, it provided a template for the cultural articulation of identity that has been adopted by later movements, such as second-wave feminism and minority ethnic groups, from Latinos to Native Americans. By providing a powerful and often combative alternative to 'mainstream' American identity, the BAM helped kick open the space required for the continued fragmentation of cultural politics. It is hard to imagine recent political identity movements – such as Standing Rock, Me Too, Occupy and Black Lives Matter – emerging in quite the same way if not for the ground that had already been broken by the BAM. Second, the concerns and issues raised by the BAM were often actually universal rather than particular. The critique that BAM brought to bear against neo-colonialism often hinged upon injustices that were class based rather than necessarily *just* racial – it is not surprising, then, that many of the key figures within BAM gradually moved during the 1970s towards an affili-ation with Marxist–Leninist groups. The BAM therefore became more than the cultural expression of Black political consciousness, it became a dynamic and influential feature of social change within the United States. This was of course aided by the secular connotations of this as a discourse about race (as opposed to religion), which have perhaps allowed it to more easily become a part of (an often secular) left-leaning mainstream culture and media.

In contrast, CCM was always more internally conflicted, as a move-ment and subculture, about the aims and values of the movement. While there were those who advocated Christian evangelical separateness – that which has been termed 'Christ against culture' – there were always others who pushed for access to mainstream audiences by virtue of their art. Musicians such as Kevin Smith, from DC Talk, and Amy Grant both presented themselves as serious artists, with deeply personal albums, resonating on a human rather than simply a Christian level. In contrast, musicians such as Leslie Phillips rallied evangelical Christian audiences by railing against those outside that sacred circle, with lyrics attacking the 'dull morality' of wider American culture. These two approaches are seemingly contradictory. An attempt on the one hand to make Christianity relevant for all, set against a desire, on the other hand, to keep evangelical Christians distinct and separate from the world. Yet these two approaches share something in common – they have largely left American society unchanged. CCM has either been a part of dominant musical trends – reinforcing rather than opposing – or it has offered a piercing critique of wider social morality, but only as a rallying cry for other evange-licals. Both these approaches have been successful – and CCM remains a multi-billion dollar industry with large audiences and successful institutions – but they have done so by offering a spiritual alternative to conventional morality rather than by actively levelling a political critique *against it*.

British Muslim artists are of course not unaware of these kinds of dilemmas and it is instructive to consider the ways in which they are already being dealt with by prominent Muslim artists and cultural producers. The musician Sami Yusuf is an example of the way in which labelling can become confining despite the intentions and efforts of the artist in question. A global star, Yusuf, is classically trained in both Western and Middle Eastern music styles. His first album, *Al-Mu'allim*, in 2003, combined these musical forms to produce beautiful nasheeds, often sung in Arabic, and clearly aimed at a Muslim audience. Supported by an Islamic record company, Awakening Records, Yusuf subsequently rose to prominence with a series of albums, selling millions of copies around the world. The stylistic significance of these albums was borne out by the merging of musical traditions and an attempt to voice Islamic religious themes in an accessible way for an English-speaking Muslim audience. However, over the last 10 years, he has attempted to move towards a more generic form of spiritual music that, while underpinned by his faith, is more open to a non-Muslim audience – he has termed this approach 'spiritique'. Yet because of his earlier labelling as a 'Muslim musician' and a nasheed artist – and because of his ascent to success through an almost entirely Muslim audience – he has struggled to significantly break beyond the confines of an 'Islamic' music scene.

The actor Riz Ahmed is another prominent British Muslim artist, but one who has taken a different path to Sami Yusuf. Ahmed began his career in the early to mid-2000s, with a series of performances that, while critically notable, were shaped by a post-9/11 wave of film and drama that focused on terrorism and the securitisation of Muslims. Despite obvious talent and a versatility in acting, Ahmed was known for his roles as 'a Muslim' in productions such as *The Road to Guantanamo* (2006), *Four Lions* (2010) and *The Reluctant Fundamentalist* (2013). Yet, while proud of these features, Ahmed has long been uncomfortable with appearing in roles that are determined by his ethnicity and faith. He has written eloquently about the need for minority actors to push back against the constraints of typecasting, suggesting that these roles are 'a necklace of labels to hang around your neck, neither of your choosing nor making, both constrictive and decorative'.[5] After years of trying to shatter this glass ceiling, Ahmed has subsequently broken through with roles in films such as *Nightcrawler* (2014), the Star Wars spin-off, *Rogue One* (2016) and comic-book blockbuster, *Venom* (2018) – in each of these films, Ahmed plays a character that has nothing to do with either his ethnicity or religious background. Yet it is this success – as 'just' an actor – that has provided him with the space and prominence to speak out on a range of issues (such as Islamophobia and racial profiling) that are relevant for Muslims and those from an ethnic minority background. Ahmed has also become a cultural icon for many Muslims in Britain, with prominent speaking slots at events such as London's *Eid in the Square*.

Concluding Thoughts: A British Muslim Arts Movement

So how might these comparisons help us think about a British Muslim Arts Movement? Muslim involvement in arts and culture in Britain is diverse and varied – so it is important not to overgeneralise – but as with BAM and CCM, there are a series of overlapping aims that characterise these movements, including, for example, the notion of providing an alternative, developing a social critique, religious mobilisation, political education, the development of a new aesthetic, etc. Yet, as I have shown, there can also be unintended consequences beyond the original hopes and ambitions of those involved. The BAM failed to mould an independent and isolated African American culture, but it did radically influence wider American society. Conversely, CCM failed to break out into mainstream music culture, but it has succeeded in helping to sustain and enrich a vibrant evangelical Christian community. In thinking about these examples in relation to the idea of a British Muslim Arts Movement, it is helpful to consider the questions that I posed at the beginning:

First, to what extent might an independent cultural economy help or hinder British Muslim art and culture? There can be enormous benefits in developing bespoke institutions and networks, as well as in building a unique and targeted audience. These resources can provide support, finance, capital and a platform for the dissemination of artistic work, and they can provide creative hubs that bring artists together in the development of new techniques and practices. But they can also be limiting: an affiliation with niche institutions, networks and audiences can inhibit access to new and more diverse audiences. Part of the issue for a British Muslim Arts movement is that there are many sources of 'Muslim' funding and institutional support – particularly the platforms provided by Islamic charities and *da'wah* organisations – but it is worth considering the extent to which this support, while helpful for emerging artists, might ultimately suppress future attempts to appeal to a non-Muslim audience.

Second, does recognition of a British Muslim Arts Movement necessarily assume that there is such a thing as British Muslim art? The two are not necessarily the same. A network of Muslim artists in the UK – perhaps grappling with related themes, issues and influences – does not necessarily require that there must be something so specific and potentially confining as the label 'British Muslim art'. There is of course a heritage of Islamic art, just as there are more contemporary, continuing evolutions of global Muslim culture. The point is not to dispute these influences, but to ask whether they crystallise into a specific and definable aesthetic. This is an open question and there are a range of views among different artists. But regardless of whether any such aesthetic is actually labelled, there is a privileged position to be played by British

Muslim artists in drawing on the influences of Islamic art and global Muslim culture for the benefit of others – everything from Arab science fiction and Malaysian pop music, through to classical arabesque and calligraphy. An ability to synthesise this overlooked cultural reservoir is perhaps one of the more distinctive roles that might be played by a British Muslim Arts Movement.

Third, how might a British Muslim Arts Movement develop a distinctive social and political critique? Is this critique developed in the form of an alternative – a *halal* or spiritual offering – that acts as a critical rejection of secular culture? We can witness this approach in examples such as the very successful nasheed industry. Or might a critique be developed along more direct political lines, tackling issues such as Islamophobia and securitisation for a wider audience? We might look towards cultural outputs such as the film *Freesia* (2017), aimed at a general audience, which grapples with Islamophobic violence and the motivations of the far right. Both approaches are valid and serve a purpose, but any coherent and specifically labelled arts movement might struggle to hold them together. Or put another way, it is difficult to be both removed from *and* in critical dialogue with wider society.

Ultimately, these questions drive at a deeper underlying query about the aims and purpose of a British Muslim Arts Movement. Is it attempting to transform Muslim consciousness, promote Islamic religiosity, or shape British society? It can do all three, but perhaps not at the same time.

Notes

1 John H. Bracey Jr, Sonia Sanchez, and James Smethurst. *SOS – Calling All Black People: A Black Arts Movement Reader*. Boston, MA: University of Massachusetts Press, 2014. James Smethurst. *The Black Arts Movement: Literary Nationalism in the 1960s and 1970s*. Chapel Hill: University of North Carolina Press, 2006.
2 Jay R. Howard and John M. Streck. *Apostles of Rock: The Splintered World of Contemporary Christian Music*. Lexington, KY: University Press of Kentucky, 2015. Charlie Peacock. *At the Crossroads: An Insider's Look at the Past, Present, and Future of Contemporary Christian Music*. Nashville, TN: Broadman & Holman, 1999.
3 Maulana Karenga. *Kwanzaa: A Celebration of Family, Community and Culture*. Los Angeles, California: University of Sankore Press, 1998.
4 Paul C. Taylor. *Black is Beautiful: A Philosophy of Black Aesthetics*. Chichester: Wiley Blackwell, 2016.
5 Riz Ahmed. 'Typecast as a Terrorist'. In Nikesh Shukla (ed.) *The Good Immigrant*. London: Cornerstone, 2016, p. 60.

2 Decentring the Colonial Gaze

The Framing of Islamic Art

Shaheen Kasmani

Islamic Art has a recognisable visual identity that transcends time and place, as well as differences in languages and culture. It conveys an underlying spirituality, which gives it a remarkable coherence, regardless of the country or time in which it was created. Aesthetically, it is defined by three elements: calligraphy, geometry, and *islimi* (biomorphic patterns) which will be discussed later. Many of the areas from which this art originates were colonised by European powers, and colonial legacies continue to affect how we discuss and appreciate a traditional spiritual art form. Examples of this include how Islamic Art is or isn't acknowledged as an art form, written about, categorised and how it is displayed in museums and galleries – often completely decontextualised and without any explanation of underlying spirituality. In this piece, I want to draw attention to the way Islamic Art has been racialised and colonised and explore how as Muslims we may reclaim our shared heritage.

What does decentring mean, and what is decoloniality? My understanding is that it is a confrontation of colonial legacy and white supremacy, which does not hide behind the tokenistic and repetitive conversations around diversity. It is also speaking truth to power, and reclaiming, revealing and being honest about a historical legacy that informs our context today. Above all, it is the giving back, returning, or reclaiming of land, resources, power and agency. For example, decentring could include museums being honest about their collections, and how they have produced their own decontextualised knowledge of it, resulting in epistemicides and new enforced epistemologies. It is about removing the white gaze from what we are doing/thinking/seeing, and instead self-determining in the face of Eurocentric domination. In real terms, it means the repatriation of resources and objects, as well as land. Colonisation did not just mean occupation, theft, genocide and rape, but it also defined what is culture, what is art, what is worthy and what is valuable; it institutionalised how to consider art, how to appreciate it and how to define it and produce epistemologies, methodologies and theories about it. And if that is done through Eurocentric frameworks,

DOI: 10.4324/9781003330714-4

which it undoubtedly is, we're also talking about racialisation and Orientalism, and the very image we have of ourselves.

For as long as supremacy and colonialism have been around, so have decolonial movements and struggles led by indigenous peoples around the world. These are well-established traditions that have produced impactful work well before the term decolonial became fashionable amongst western institutions, who use it in a flippant and tokenistic way. Some thinkers and writers include Edward Said, Franz Fanon, bell hooks, Malcolm X, Ngugi Wa Thiongo, Arundhati Roy, Assata Shakur, Angela Davis, and contemporary movements include Rhodes Must Fall, Fees Must Fall, Why is My Curriculum White amongst many others. However, decolonising does not mean holding on to nostalgia of the 'golden age' or trying to restore the pre-colonial, which would be impossible and even then, the past has also been framed in terms of hierarchy and language. To decolonise is to confront the past and challenge our contemporary context. To undo colonisation, if that is possible.

Whilst a lot of this chapter is about definitions and trying to define art, it is perhaps ironic that I do believe it is something transcendental and incredibly difficult to define. Islamic art has evolved and accrued meaning and form over time and space. Principally, it is about reminding the onlooker about Allah, where we come from, and where we will return to. Like many cultures and traditions, in early Muslim societies, there was no differentiation between art and craft, even everyday objects were made to last with the highest skills. We are told that God is beautiful and loves beauty[1] and that everything we do should be done with excellence.[2] Muslim artists and architects have taken this quite literally! Islam teaches us that everything can be a form of worship if done with the right intention and that would include making art. It may often look like abstract patterns but is not always without meaning or significance as some contemporary European geometrists would have us believe.[3] Hence the need to decentre Eurocentric thought and theory.

As I mentioned previously, Islamic Art (see Figure 2.1) is aesthetically made up of three elements[4] – probably the most iconic is calligraphy (Figure 2.2), often the written word of Allah (but also hadith, poetry, etc.). It is considered the highest art form in not just technical skill but sacredness, as it is often the word of Allah in physically scripted form. Imam Ali ibn Abi Talib is quoted to have said that 'The beauty of writing is the tongue of the hand and the elegance of thought'.[5] Geometric patterns perhaps the most ubiquitous are derived from circles and straight lines that signify the depiction of space, time and our place in the universe (see Figure 2.3). The patterns found in Islamic geometry are the same patterns found in nature, on the macro level such as the relationship and movement between planets, to the measurement of branches on a tree or leaves on a stem, down to the micro, the number patterns found in our own bodies and cells. For example, many geometric patterns visually explore the Fibonacci sequence, which is

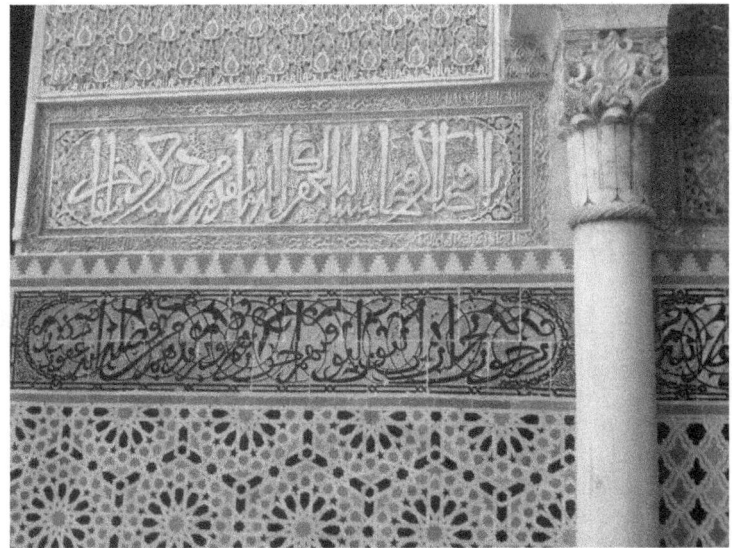

Figure 2.1 An image of the Ben Attarine Madrasa in Fes, Morocco.
Source: Shaheen Kasmani.

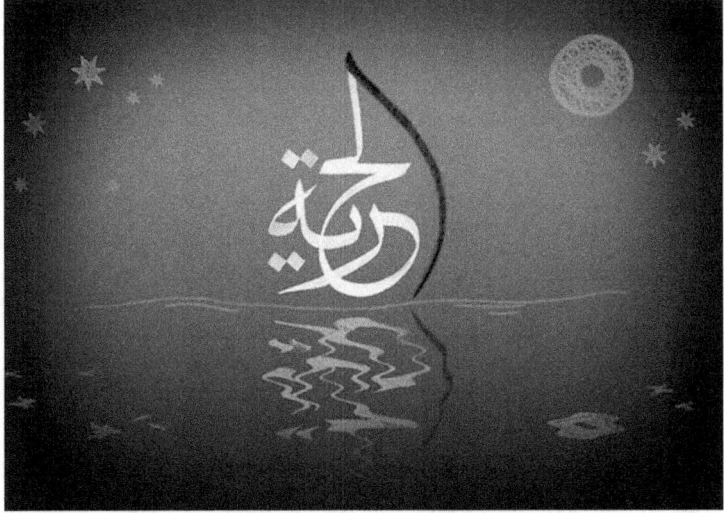

Figure 2.2 Hurriyah by Soraya Syed.
Source: Soraya Syed.

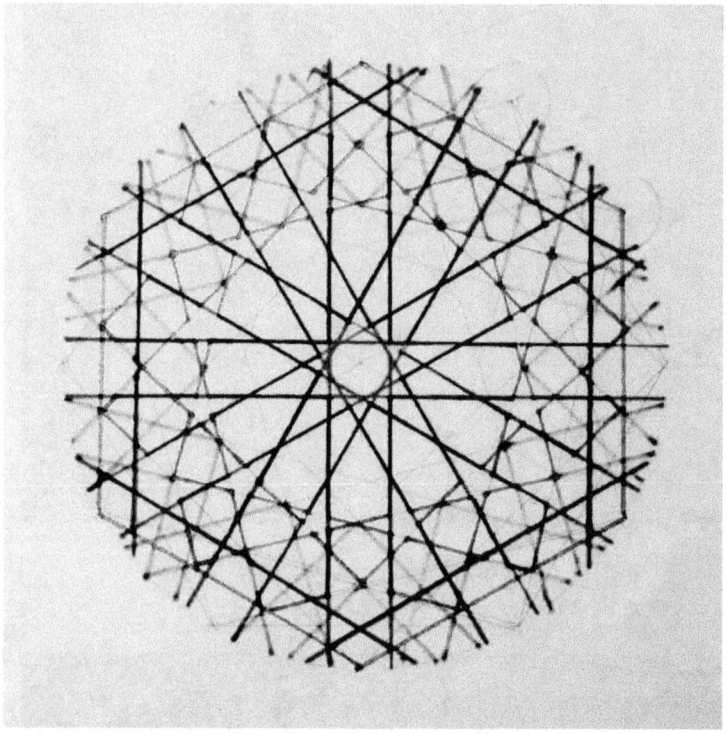

Figure 2.3 A construction drawing of a 12-fold geometric rosette pattern found in
   the Alhambra in Granada, Spain.

Source: Shaheen Kasmani.

also found in the growth patterns of the natural world, and Islamic architecture and manuscript layouts are often based around the golden ratio.[6]

The third element is *islimi* (biomorphic) – unrealistic and stylised floral
designs and spirals that serve as a reminder of paradise, unrealistic because
we do not know what Jannah actually looks like (see Figure 2.4). The leaves
and flowers are not exactly like what we see in nature, but inspired by it. As
Syed Hossein Nasr says, 'Islamic Art does not imitate the actual forms of
nature, but reflects the principles' and is based on rhythm, balance and
harmony.[7] For example, in Ottoman iznik patterns, the elongated tulip
(Figure 2.5) is said to symbolise supplication to Allah,[8] as hands raised
upwards, and the rose a symbol of the Prophet (peace be upon him).[9]
Visually, Islamic art can be one, two or three of these elements, but I also
feel that it could be none, depending of course on the message, or the

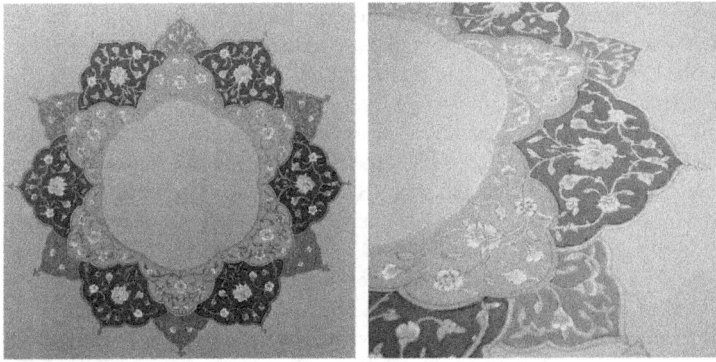

Figure 2.4 A shamsa (small sun) painted in the Persian style, painted by Shaheen Kasmani.

Source: Shaheen Kasmani.

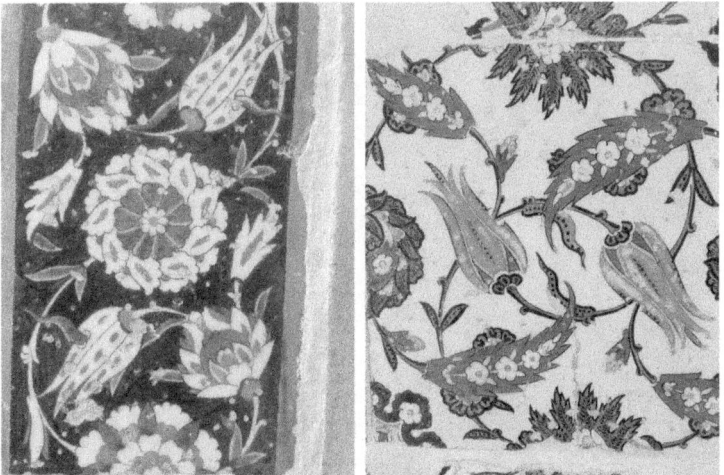

Figure 2.5 Photos of tiles from the Eyup Sultan mosque and Topkapi Palace, Istanbul.

Source: Shaheen Kasmani.

narrative behind the work. If art is something that directs the heart or mind towards Oneness of God, could it be considered Islamic Art? Conceptually, it is there to remind you to contemplate nature, creation, our own selves and the Creator the most High. It is about harmony, pointing to Tawheed – that there is One God, from which everything comes and to which every- thing returns, hence all patterns, however complex, are derived from a single circle and can be traced back to the centre point of that same circle.

Scholars such as Laleh Bakhtiar, Syed Hossein Nasr, Titus Burkhardt and Martin Lings[10] have written extensively about the symbolism of Islamic art, from the meaning of specific shapes in geometry and their significance to the abjad number system[11] and links to the cosmos. For example, when you see an eight-pointed star (Figure 2.6) which is ubiquitous to Islamic art and architecture all over the world, it is considered a reference to the eight angels that hold up the throne of Allah (Surah al Haqqah, verse 69) and the

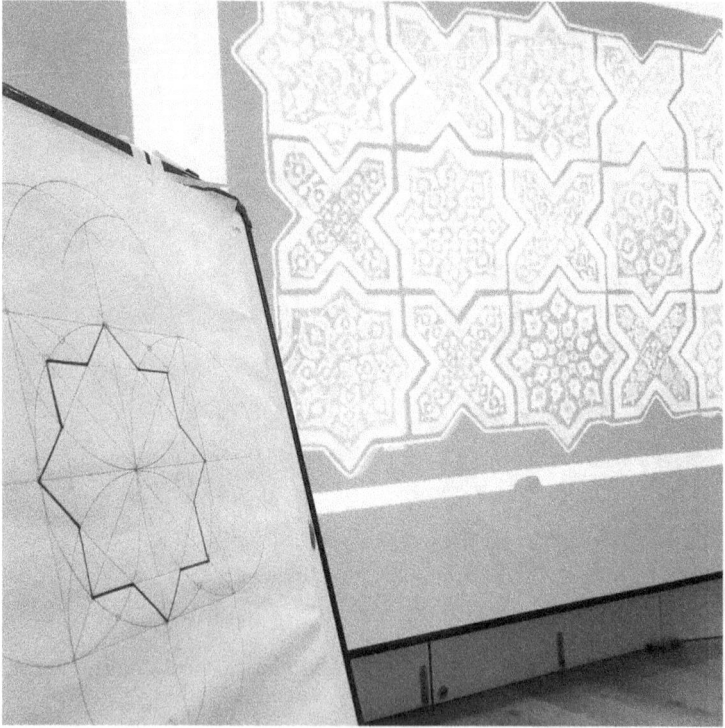

Figure 2.6 Eight-pointed star and its geometric construction from a class taught by Shaheen Kasmani.

Source: Shaheen Kasmani.

eight gates to Jannah – a reminder of what we are aiming for. A pattern of repeating eight-pointed stars has come to be known as 'breath of the compassionate' because with its underlying grid of intersecting circles, it is endless – like Allah's mercy itself.[12]

However, these specific geometric patterns have accrued meaning over time and were not used at the time of the Prophet, or in the building of the first mosque by the Prophet in Medina (Figure 2.7). As Islam spread, it adapted to local artistic cultures and traditions, which can be seen in mosque architecture. For example, contrast the Grand Mosque in Xian which was built during the Hongwu reign of the Ming dynasty (1368–1398), with the great mosque of Djenne in Mali, built in 1902. Both are incredibly different and faithful to their environment, yet both serve the same purpose; a place to worship God as a community. Mosque architecture around the world is another way to demonstrate the principle of multiplicity towards unity. Many mosques in the regions of Syria and Palestine also adapted some of the architectural styles of basilicas, churches and synagogues, and whilst there are some core differences between the faiths, architecture remains a visual reminder of the commonalities.[13] We also see similar crossovers in Spain, Portugal and Italy, where architecture, including sacred spaces like churches and synagogues, clearly incorporate what are recognisable Islamic geometric patterns. This serves as yet another example of how shifting the framework around art and architecture is needed in our understanding of histories of societies and relationships of creativity, and a deeper understanding of art history, and why these patterns flow between

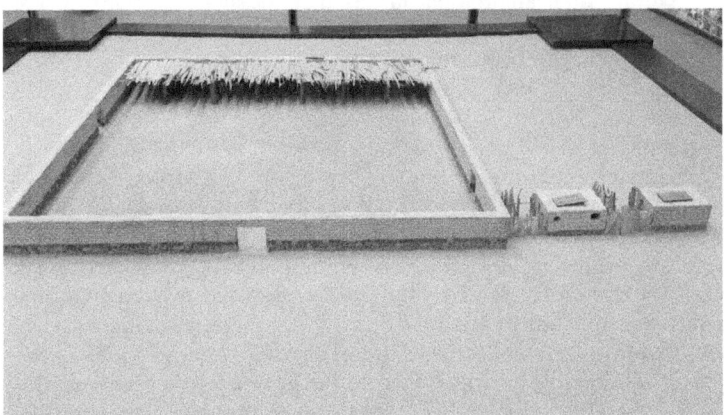

Figure 2.7 A photo of a model of the first mosque in Medina, built by the Prophet Muhammed (pbuh) and his companions.

Source: Shaheen Kasmani.

sacred spaces of different faiths, as well as the disruptions and discrimination inflicted by those in power.

Islamic Art, and indeed sacred art, places the Divine at its centre, although this is not visually depicted in Islamic Art as Muslims believe that God cannot be contained in material form. Many art historians are under the impression that the patterns and abstraction in Islamic Art are due to the prohibition of human and animal figures, which seems simplistic and reductive. Of course, there are sources where the depiction of human forms is discouraged and in some cases prohibited, but we also see people and animals beautifully painted in early manuscripts, such as Mughal and Persian manuscript paintings.

Islamic Art would also be different to a term I have heard recently, 'Muslim art' – art made by someone who happens to be Muslim (but may or may not be making what we might consider to be Islamic art) and may or may not be about contesting Muslims' place in society. But where has this new label come from, and why does it matter? There are ongoing wider debates about a specific Muslim identity being created as a response to misrecognition and misrepresentation. With focus on the superficial, gendered Islamophobia and nonsensical hijab and burka bans, we do not have the same labels like Jewish artist and Hindu artist, unless the art that is made is of a theological nature and in a specific context. Artists of other faiths and none are not asked to demonstrate their identities in the same way; there is way too much art that is promoted simply because it is about hijab, and the image of, or art about hijab has also been co-opted as a tokenistic gesture of inclusivity. The rising culture of Islamophobia means that Muslims, even in our creativity, are under the anthropological and ethnographic spotlight, and something 'other' to be scrutinised and studied.

An example of this is an arts project, funded through the UK government's 'Prevent' counter-extremism programme, that a group of artists were asked to deliver in a primary school in Alum Rock, Birmingham.[14] The student body of the school in question is majority Muslim, living in a deprived area of the city. The objective of the art workshops was to collectively produce three mini murals that were based on Islamic *islimi* designs, combining florals, vines, leaves and spirals. However, funded by the Home Office, but delivered through second- and third-party organisations, this was the guise under which those involved were collecting data on children without their consent or their parents' permission. One of the external organisations asked students to fill in a questionnaire with their opinions on living in the UK, gender roles, race and religion and educational aspirations[15] – nothing to do with the art itself.[16] Not only does this raise questions about violations of the children's rights under Article 8 of the European Convention and under the Data Protection Act, but it also uses a sacred art form in an insidious way, as a tool for discreet data collection, and the demonisation and securitisation of Muslim children. In this particular example, when art facilitators asked the school staff how they had chosen children for the arts activity, they were told that the children chosen were those 'with the strongest opinions'.

The encroachment of Prevent, and the wider logic of the War on Terror,[17] on the arts in general and Islamic art in particular is a truly colonial approach; it divides communities under the pretence of culture and creativity and creates a version of the 'native informant' though the artist, which is truly dangerous, and in complete opposition to the essence and intention of sacred art. It could also be argued that the use of sacred art for this purpose is a form of spiritual abuse; art which is normally the realm of expression, exploration, storytelling and experimentation is now used as a means of surveillance, inevitably breeding further mistrust and divisions, and in this case is targeting Muslims, but is ultimately an attack on civil liberties for all. Will art be used to monitor all those who voice political difference and dissent? When funding is scarce and education budgets for the arts are being cut drastically, free arts activities made available for schools on this premise are duplicitous. That is unless, leadership in such schools is of the same opinion that Muslims are to be suspected, which shows how subjective the Prevent policy is. Using the arts in such a way suggests that there is a correlation between art activities and de/radicalisation, which has been written about extensively by Suhaiymah Manzoor-Khan.[18]

In her review of the Trojan Horse Affair podcast by New York Times journalists Brian Reed and Hamza Syed, Dr Khadijah Elshayyal reflects that a far-reaching impact of the Trojan Hoax affair is the killing off of imagination, and the aspiration to achieve.[19] Gendered, structural and systemic Islamophobia took a group of schools in one of Birmingham's most deprived and ignored areas, with a majority Kashmiri Pakistani Muslim population, from good and outstanding to special measures overnight.[20] So whilst people may not have actually died, careers ended and state violence killed off the hopes, dreams and imaginations of so many children and their teachers. The Prevent policy is a direct result of the Trojan Hoax affair, and in schools it is now using art and creativity, an area that is otherwise so freeing and life-affirming, to do just that.

In museums, collections of objects that come under the broad categorisation of Islamic/Asian/African art are extensive and well looked after and often curated for specialist exhibitions. They are auctioned for hundreds of thousands, even millions of pounds, celebrated, conserved and lauded for the technical skill involved in their making as well as their beauty. But again, here we see an imposed narrative; there have been a few recent articles on how Islamic art can be used to counter the extremist 'bad Muslim' narrative, and it is dehumanising.[21] Are the articles really saying that 'If they created something so beautiful, they can't all be that bad can they? It is being used as something to which we are again, being asked to prove ourselves against, in order to humanise ourselves. And if I, because I am Muslim, am being asked to prove myself as a human, then the person or institution asking me to do this has already decided that I am not. As soon as this is part of the discourse we are on dangerous ground, and othered to quite an extreme. And this does not take into account socio-economic boundaries and borders, geopolitics, violence and rising Islamophobia, and European history has shown us how this story can start, develop and continue.

In museums and art galleries, the art is celebrated, but so detached from its context, it almost becomes devoid of meaning. Sacred objects, or those objects that have sacred significance, are reduced to their materiality and time scale. For example, a manuscript of the Qur'an with Arabic calligraphy will generally not have the translation of the verses, or the context of the revelation on the museum label.[22] At most, we may get a verse reference. Its very purpose has been redefined, as an art history object and not something that is sacred – and more often than not, by those who are not Muslim, and are very distant from Muslim communities. Additionally, when art is discussed in museum and gallery spaces, it is alluded to in a very Orientalist way; objects are often displayed in a 'cabinet of curiosities'. They are decontextualised from their original purposes, as well as how they came about to be in western museums. The fragmentation of the narrative around the art is emphasised when art categorised as Islamic, such as manuscript paintings, is referred to as being Sufi in nature, as Sufism is often considered to be the more palatable, softer, 'poetry-about-wine version of Islam'. However, the principles of Sufism play a central role in mainstream Islamic orthodoxy, and one cannot be a Sufi without being a Muslim first. Framing discourses in such a way erases the diversity of creativity, practice and privileges within Muslim communities.

Furthermore, museums and galleries, although many claim to be, are not neutral spaces and do not want to confront how sacred objects are displayed in secular environments.[23] When displaying stolen loot from India, or Egypt, or any other former British colony, the institution sets the framework from which the object is viewed, and its frameworks are undoubtedly Eurocentric. The narrative around the art is defined and the agenda is already set. Many of the curators of Islamic Art collections are not Muslims themselves, so may inevitably disregard the spiritual or sacred significance of what's on display. Those who do have this knowledge, be they individuals or communities, are either not credited or remunerated for the intellectual labour, or employed for any length of time. The colonial space uses colonial means to keep things in, and people out.[24]

It is also racialised – how often, when discussing Islamic art, do we focus on the modern-day Middle East, North Africa and The Indian Subcontinent. Most exhibition displays focus on these areas, and whilst museums do hold extensive collections of art from the African continent, how often do they go on display? How many of us are aware of the rich heritage of Islamic art and architecture found in provinces of China or places like Timbuktu in Mali, or Zanzibar off the coast of east Africa? This does us a disservice; our interconnectedness as a community, as an ummah, breaks down without this mutual recognition, appreciation and sense of heritage. And not in a way that means ownership or co-option, but appreciation and gratitude. But without this education, does that not feed into the anti-blackness we see, in society in general and in our communities? It is an artistic and spiritual global heritage, and in the way the ummah is described by the Prophet, that matters. If art, architecture, history, literature and music are marks of a community and their legacy, and I strongly believe that art is the way we reflect our contexts, then we must question how we see ourselves, and through whose gaze? It is gendered too; there is a documented history of Muslim women calligraphers, which seems to be forgotten and overlooked.[25] Today, we sadly seem to have aligned values with the mainstream art world where those who get the most space and recognition are white men.

When art is taken away from its context and is secularised, it loses its essence and revolutionary potential. For example, William Morris, canonical in English design and heritage and lauded with reviving the design industry in England, is celebrated in museums all over the country as well as his own in east London. He derives much of his work and design style from Islamic and Indian patterns.[26] According to the V&A website, William Morris found inspiration in the ordered patterns of Islamic art and particularly admired the magnificent Ardabil Carpet, which is the V&A's largest and most famous piece of Islamic art.[27] This is hardly ever referenced or mentioned in work about him. In an exhibition at Birmingham Museum Art Gallery in 2016, Morris' other influences, experiences and political beliefs were cited, but the exhibition failed to mention one of his most important inspirations. A huge oversight from the curator and the museum. Can we consider this as one of the earlier examples of cultural/appropriation? There is a contemporary colonisation of the art form – from Iraqi relics in the British Museum that somehow arrived there after Bush and Blair's invasion, which includes everything from furniture to clothing and accessories with 'tribal', 'ethnic' and geometric designs.

What I have noticed is the complete whitewashing of Islamic art. There are many artists who are undoubtedly talented geometers, but claim that the art has no spiritual or sacred meaning, that it is just extremely clever visual maths. Many are not Muslims themselves but have enforced their own secularisation on the art. I do not believe that one has to be Muslim to practice or even specialise in this art form, because that then also brings into question religiosity of Muslim artists, but there is a need to acknowledge a tradition and respect its sacred principles. Whilst the symbolism of geometric patterns and architectural features is debatable, the art history is not recorded in a way that western academia recognises and is therefore often dismissed. This is another example of how we need to decolonise our view, by decentring the coloniser and instead centring the art itself.

By decentring God, something else takes its place. Individuals have instead centred themselves as artists and creators, and like most things we have an issue with – it is pale, male and stale, and making a profit. It is being repackaged and sold back to us. An imposed capitalist secularism means that something is lost in the process, and decontextualises the art from its heritage, its history and its meaning. We see this in high street stores, on clothing and soft furnishings that were mass produced in unsafe environments in factories in places like Bangladesh, drastically polluting the environment and not paying workers adequate wages, or providing safe working environments.

In my own art, and own practice, and as a Muslim who believes in the sacred, I feel like I can have a certain legitimacy.[28] I play with the forms and express them, but this is only possible when the underlying principles are understood and appreciated. It is contextual, there was (and still is) a time when saying that there is only one God was a revolutionary statement, and this art remains a reminder of that. Now, speaking in our context, Islam teaches us to speak truth to power,[29] and it is our duty to do so by choosing our medium, and this is mine. Perhaps I am repurposing it for today, but as Nina Simone said, the role of an artist is to reflect the times in which they find themselves.[30] People claim that the same patterns are being reproduced again and again and that the art form is in stasis. But again, whose voice gets platformed and who gets to define what is and is not worthy of art? Perhaps the patterns and designs are being reworked, but there is also a lot of innovation and experimentation (for example, see the work of Zarah Hussain playing with light and 3d forms, Dr Sara Chaudhry, and the work of Sara Al-Abdali, as well as calligrapher Soraya Syed and illuminator Ayesha Gamiet).[31] The stories are different, and it is the reclaiming of that narrative for ourselves, and the revolutionary nature of art, especially as a Muslim woman, which I find imperative for the future. Art spaces are also changing. Artist collectives are coming together to cater for each other and the community by building networks, raising funds and facilitating their own art exhibitions and creative events.[32] This in itself is changing the conversation around art, who gets to define it, and who gets to approve it.

This chapter is an initial piece of research and exploration, which through my own practice as an artist, questions what decentring and decoloniality are, what they mean, and how we approach these ideas culturally and artistically. The ways in which western museums and galleries display (or indeed, do not display) Islamic art needs challenging, I am not sure it is possible to decolonise, as that would mean repatriating all of the objects and an almost empty building. What we do need to confront is how the art is considered, valued and framed, both physically on display and theoretically. We also need to consider our definitions of Islamic Art – are they too binary and too stringent? Especially as art can be transient and universal, as the principles behind Islamic art are. Artists and creative collectives, such as those mentioned above, are decentring the colonial gaze, and reframing narratives, which is something that needs to be supported and championed for generations to come, as well as the conversation around art itself.

To me, Islamic art is a way of expressing my faith and political views in a time when words are not sufficient. If we do not own our art, and who we are, we will be owned. One of my favourite writers, Toni Morrison, said that 'definitions belong to the definers, not the defined' and for many of us, we are deciding on our own definitions.[33]

Notes

1 From 'Abdullah ibn Mas'ud *radiallahu 'anhu* who said that the Prophet *sallallahu 'alayhi wa sallam* said, "No one will enter Paradise who has an atom's weight of pride in his heart." A man said, "What if a man likes his clothes to look good and his shoes to look good?" He said, *"Allah is beautiful and loves beauty. Pride means denying the truth and looking down on people."* Related by Muslim, Riyadh as Saliheen, The Book of Miscellany, Book 1, Hadith 612, https://sunnah.com/riyadussaliheen/1/612 [accessed 30 September 2019].

2 '*Ihsan*' in the Quran, often translated as 'excellence' or 'good'/'goodness'. See translations of 4:36 and 2:195 in M.A.S Abdul Haleem, Oxford: Oxford University Press, 2015; Abdullah Yusuf Ali, Kitab Bhavan, 2001; Mohammad Asad, The Book Foundation, 2008.

3 Erig Broug. 'Too Much Reverance?' Presentation to CIADA 2015 Conference, Singapore, 2015: https://www.youtube.com/watch?v=e3FecGGOnz0 [accessed 30 September 2019].

4 Ed Khaled Azzam. *Arts and Crafts of Islamic Lands: Principles, Materials, Practice.* London: Thames & Hudson, 2013.

5 Seyyed Hossein Nasr. *Islamic Art and Spirituality.* New York: SUNY Press, 1987, p. 17.

6 The golden ratio is a mathematical pattern in which a line is cut so that the shorter section is to the longer as the longer is to the whole line (approximately 1.618). See Daud Sutton. *Islamic Design.* London: Wooden Books, 2007, p. 36.

7 Seyyed Hossein Nasr. *Islamic Art and Spirituality.* New York: SUNY Press, 1987, p. 8.

8 Ismail Karakelle. *Rustem Pasha Mosque and Iznik Tiles*, 2nd Edition. Cemre Ajans, 2011.

9 Seyyed Hossein Nasr. *Islamic Art and Spirituality.* New York: SUNY Press, 1987.

10 Laleh Bakhtiar. *Sufi: Expressions of the Mystic Quest*. London: Thames & Hudson, 1976; Martin Lings. *Symbol and Archetype: A Study of the Meaning of Existence*. Fons Vitae, 2005; Seyyed Hossein Nasr. *Islamic Art and Spirituality*. New York: SUNY Press, 1987; Titus Burkhardt. *Art of Islam: Language and Meaning*. Bloomington, IN: World Wisdom Books, 2009. Titus Burkhardt. *Sacred Art in East and West*. Perennial Books, 1967.

11 This is a system in which Arabic letters are assigned a numeric value. After adopting the Indian decimal numerals, these letters had symbolic meaning attached to them also. See Daud Sutton. *Islamic Design: A Genius for Geometry*. London: Wooden Books, 2007, p. 37. It has been claimed that this system has talismanic qualities, however this notion has faced the religious objection that the idea contradicts the tawheedic principle of relying on Allah alone, as well as the secular objection that it promotes orientalist narratives advances by institutions such as museums and places of higher education.

12 Laleh Bakhtiar. *Sufi: Expressions of the Mystic Quest*. London: Thames & Hudson, 1976, p. 16; Daud Sutton. *Islamic Design: A Genius for Geometry*. London: Wooden Books, 2007, p. 8.

13 For example, the Umayyad Mosque in Damascus, Syria.

14 For more information on the Prevent policy see: National Union of Students, *Preventing Prevent Handbook*. London: National Union of Students, 2017: https://www.nusconnect.org.uk/resources/preventing-prevent-handbook [accessed 17 September 2019]; and Suhaiymah Manzoor-Khan. 'Statement on Building a Stronger Britain Together (Counter Extremism) Fund and withdrawal from Bradford Literature Festival'. *The Brow Hijabi*, 17 June 2019: https://thebrownhijabi.com/2019/07/01/statement-on-building-a-stronger-britain-together-counter-extremism-fund-and-withdrawal-from-bradford-literature-festival-full-text/ [accessed 17 September 2019].

15 This inclusion of educational aspirations is deeply ironic given that counter-extremism interventions in Birmingham – especially the so-called "Trojan Horse" scandal, which saw several Birmingham schools accused by the UK government of being involved in an "Islamist plot" – have had deleterious impacts upon school achievement. See John Holmwood and Therese O'Toole. *Countering Extremism in British Schools: The Truth about the Birmingham Trojan Horse Affair*. Policy Press, 2018.

16 The full case study and copy of the questionnaire can be found at: Open Society Justice Initiative. *Eroding Trust: The UK's Prevent Counter-Extremism Strategy in Health and Education*. New York: Open Society Foundations: https://www.justiceinitiative.org/publications/eroding-trust-uk-s-prevent-counter-extremism-strategy-health-and-education [accessed 17 September 2019].

17 On art and the War on Terror see Jessica Winegar. "The Humanity Game: Art, Islam, and the War on Terror." *Anthropological Quarterly* 81, no. 3 (2008): 651–81. https://doi.org/10.1353/anq.0.0024.

18 Suhaiymah Manzoor-Khan and Saima Mir. 'Does Bradford Festival's Counter-Extremism Funding Warrant a Boycott?' *The Guardian*, 24 June 2019: https://www.theguardian.com/commentisfree/2019/jun/24/bradford-literary-festival-counter-extremism-funding-boycott [accessed 21 July 2022].

19 Khadijah Elshayyal. 'Swim or Sink: The Trojan Horse Affair as a Witch-Hunt of the Forever "Underclass"'. *Amaliah*, 25 February 2022: https://www.amaliah.com/post/64099/trojan-horse-affair-podcast-review-prevent-strategy-muslims [accessed 21 July 2022].

20 Brian Reed and Hamza Syed. *The Trojan Horse Affair*. Podcast series. Serial
    Productions: https://www.nytimes.com/interactive/2022/podcasts/trojan-
    horse-affair.html [accessed 21 July 2022].
21 Jonathan Jones. 'The Beauty of Art can Counter Islamophobia – But it Won't
    be Easy'. *The Guardian*, 8 March 2017: https://www.theguardian.com/
    artanddesign/jonathanjonesblog/2017/mar/08/new-york-institute-arab-
    islamic-art-islamophobia [accessed 21 July 2022].
22 The Qur'ans on display at the Jameel Gallery in the V&A, for example, are
    displayed without this information.
23 Sumaya Kassim. 'The Museum is the Master's House: An Open
    Letter to Tristram Hunt'. *Medium*, 26 July 2019: https://medium.com/@
    sumayakassim/the-museum-is-the-masters-house-an-open-letter-to-tristram-
    hunt-e72d75a891c8 [accessed 21 July 2022].
24 Sumaya Kassim. 'The Museum Will Not Be Decolonised'. *Media Diversified*,
    15 November 2017: https://mediadiversified.org/2017/11/15/the-museum-will-
    not-be-decolonised/ [accessed 19 July 2022].
25 Examples are provided in: Mohammed Akram Nadwi. *Al-Muhaddithat: The
    Women Scholars of Islam*. London: Interface Publications, 2007. See also displays
    of Qur'an manuscripts in the Museum of Islamic Art in Doha, Qatar (naming
    Sultana Fatima Khatun as the calligrapher in a manuscript from Brunei, 1800).
26 Gillian Naylor. *William Morris by Himself: Designs and Writings*. London:
    Little Brown and Company, 1998, p. 12
27 Details of the Ardabil Carpet and all the V&A's 'Islamic Middle East' col-
    lection can be found at: http://www.vam.ac.uk/content/articles/p/plant-
    motifs-in-islamic-art/
28 See www.shaheenkasmani.com and www.instagram.com/shaheen.kasmani
    [accessed 19 July 2022].
29 On the authority of Abu Sa'eed Khudree, may Allah be pleased with him,
    who said: I heard the Messenger of Allah (peace and blessings of Allah be
    upon him) say "Whosoever of you sees an evil, let him change it with his
    hand; and if he is not able to do so, then let him change it with this tongue;
    and if he is not able to do so, then with his heart – and that is the weakest of
    faith" Muslim, 40 Hadith Nawawi: https://sunnah.com/nawawi40/34 [ac-
    cessed 19 July 2022].
30 Nina Simone quoted in *Nina Simone: Great Performances, College Concerts
    and Interviews*. Sound Dimensions, 2009. An excerpt of the interview can be
    found at: https://www.youtube.com/watch?v=0qL3nHvliN4 [accessed 19 July
    2022].
31 The web pages of these artists can be found at: Zarah Hussain: http://
    zarahhussain.co.uk; Sara Al-Abdali: http://www.sarahalabdali.com/; Soyaya
    Syed: https://www.artofthepen.com/; Ayesha Gamiet: http://ayeshagamiet.
    com/ [accessed 21 July 2022].
32 Examples include Variant Space: http://www.variantspace.com/; Manifesting
    the Unseen: https://www.manifestingtheunseen.com/; OOMK: http://www.
    oomk.net/; Female Muslim Creatives: https://www.instagram.com/
    femalemuslimcreatives/; Rabbits Road Press: https://www.rabbitsroadpress.
    com/; and The White Pube: https://www.thewhitepube.co.uk/ [accessed 21 July
    2022].
33 Toni Morrison. *Beloved*. Vintage, 1997, p. 225.

Part II
Art in Contemporary British Muslim Culture

3   The Nature of Islamic Art

Locating a Tradition of Fitrah in the Art and Culture of Islam, with Particular Reference to Calligraphy

Razwan ul-Haq

In the world we inhabit today, an automatic leaning towards categorising whatever surrounds us means taking an almost reductive view of existence. Some may say it is Aristotelian logic, others may assert it is a scientific, neutral and progressive way of looking at phenomena. Simply put, this particular worldview would deem it logical that Muslims would produce Art that is an outpouring of their religion. Yet others may argue that categorising Art forms of the 'conquered natives' by Western universities is a hangover from colonialism. Art done in the Western world is deemed as *Art not culturally Western* but *universalist* (hence purely artistic labels such as abstract, impressionism and minimalism are applied to contemporary Western artists) whilst other forms of art need religious, cultural or other geographic indexing. It is almost as if humans outside the modern West are only capable of creating one form, whether Aboriginal, African or Islamic. Contemporary Western Art specialists are considered simply to be experts on Art; Artists in almost any other imaginable genre are seen as particular.

But there is another view. Seyyed Hossein Nasr and others have in fact argued for the delineating of Islamic Art.[1] They have supported the idea of bringing to the world the category of 'Islamic Art'. I think this has been, and always will be, a double-edged way of perceiving Art created by Muslim Artists who are in tune with their traditions. Whilst recognising Islamic Art means that it gives an opportunity to interpret Art from a cultural, religious or spiritual lens, it also restricts what Muslim Artists 'ought' to be doing. There is, for example, a curious dichotomy that makes a distinction between Islamic Art and Muslim Art. In this line of reasoning, Muslim Art is Art done by Muslims that is not connected with Islam. Whereas Islamic Art has 'Islamic' aspects. I find this approach unnecessary and perhaps a leftover of colonial thinking. A religion that has over a billion followers will no doubt have

DOI: 10.4324/9781003330714-6

artists that would create manifold art forms. It is quite obvious that a political satirist living in Istanbul, for instance, when drawing a cartoon is drawing a cartoon. There is no need, in such circumstances to think in terms of Islamic Art/Muslim Art. When we are discussing Islamic Art, we are looking at it from a different dimension and dialectic.

Whilst it is clear Muslims themselves did not categorise their art as 'Islamic Art', and this classification has presumably only come into parlance due to the influences outside the Muslim world (and only quite recently, especially with regard to the 'modern' concept of what constitutes 'religion') I want to make a point here from empirical experience.[2] One cannot help but see the immense differences between the Muslim and the Christian approaches to Art whilst standing in the *Mezquita*. When I visited sites of the Cathedral and the Mosque in the Cordoba, I could not but note the different feelings one has when in the Christian and Muslim spaces. Perhaps there is mileage in using terms like 'Islamic Art' and 'Christian Art'.[3] However, there is a difference in the emotions when one is in a Mosque in Turkey, in Pakistan or in Spain. But do they have commonalities? Is there a point in searching for them? As someone who often delivers talks and workshops to Art students, I would say there is a need to define art forms though one must bear in mind all tools of analysis have weaknesses and frames of references that do not result in unbiased conclusions.

It is on this specific point that I wish to draw away from looking at things from various points of view and gather together my particular experiences in *Makkah*. On my initial pilgrimage to *Makkah*, I noticed it was spartan. Minimalist. Why would the Divine choose a site that lay around a barren wilderness? Whilst *Makkah* is now quite developed, when I visited, the sandy desert seemed to extend right up to the gates of the *Haram Ash-Sharif*.

I don't believe in coincidences and am more of a reader of Jung.[4] I mention this in passing as I had been perusing over photographs of Japanese Zen rock gardens a day or two before visiting *Makkah*, and one picture in particular which had shown a garden full of sand and rocks. I immediately felt a sense of synchronicity inside me. The theme of minimalism and Islam was becoming increasingly clear.

As I prayed and reflected under the shade of the *Ka'ba*, thoughts would enter my mind, feelings would pour out of my heart and my pen would record them and play with them. That there was no enclosed solidity and dark shadows of the churches and makeshift mosques I had become familiar with in England struck me. And here I neither found the fantastical colours and decorations of the Mosques in Pakistan.

At the central geographic, earthy axis of Islam was minimal ornamentation. To me, somehow this emptiness lent itself to prayer, to observation, to reflection and to create an interpretation. It was not an embellished series of paintings. No musical instruments or songs would make me interpret the world through another human being's genius. There was, at the time, few of the looming buildings we see today. The minarets were far in the distance, dwarfed by dark mountains. There was almost nothing manifested, like the emptiness of the Ka'ba.

It spoke to me of an Art that is not concretised on earth. It is suggestive of a dual mode of aesthetic – one standing between what is perceived by the earthly senses and what is created in the mind's eye. There is a feeling in your heart that one is somewhere else. It does not make me focus on a particular time, or a particular century such as a *Michelangelo* or a *Rembrandt* might.

To Titus Burckhardt, this is essentially linked to nature. Burckhardt is an important figure in our discussion because of his efforts to theorise 'Islamic Art' as well as practically introduce 'Islamic Art' to the Art world and the public through seminal exhibitions in the early 70s. 'The function of Islamic art is analogous to that of virgin nature, of the desert especially, which likewise favors contemplation'.[5] Burckhardt here is supporting my own feelings expressed earlier. But he adds an intriguing observation about the abstract forms that are so common in Islam: 'instead of ensnaring the mind and dragging it into some imaginary world, [ornamentation with abstract forms] dissolves mental "coagulations", just as the contemplation of a stream of water, of a flame or of leaves trembling in the wind can detach the consciousness from its inward "idols"'.

In evoking nature, Burkhardt hits upon a central theme in Islam, that of *'fitrah'*.[6] He draws from the natural process of 'coagulation' and 'crystallisation' more than once in describing Islamic Art. He sees nature everywhere, including straight lines in patterns: 'the radiating of lines from multiple geometrical foci recalls snowflakes or ice; it gives the impression of calm and freshness'.[7] In one of his comparisons of the Mosque form to the Roman Basilica or Gothic Church, he points out the Mosque does not 'progress towards the altar' but instead treats us to another metaphor from nature: '[...] its void is like the mould or womb of a motionless and undifferentiated plenitude'.

As a Calligrapher, I feel that I live and breathe the intrinsic connection between *fitrah* and art. Calligraphy is based on natural harmony between letters. When I am writing Arabic in *Nastaliq*[8] script, I sense there is an inner nature of the script itself. This is not surprising. *Nastaliq* is said to have evolved out of observing the flight and movements of geese. I will sometimes venture out to see various birds and ducks and absorb their movements and lightness. There is as much to be learnt from their movements as there is between the space and distance of nature, greenery, horizons and landscapes. Whilst there is a direct visual connection between *Nastaliq* and the world of birds, there is also another more mystical connection between them.

Cutting a bamboo pen, making ink and paper involves a high degree of knowledge of natural processes. It is not always necessary these days to make paper but in creating inks and bamboo pens and coatings for paper I attempt to use natural and local materials wherever possible. When I make my inks, I include the natural aroma of flowers. There is a tradition amongst some calligraphers to grow roses and other flowers. I have noticed how my work changes when I am closer to nature or away from it.

Some people on looking at my work may not immediately see the nature in it. I sometimes use automobiles and space scenes and to an observer, the *fitrah* element may not always seem apparent. But I think that when the onlooker finds the calligraphy of the Lamborghini (see Figure 3.1) appealing they often don't realise how the harmony inherent in calligraphy has been juxtaposed with the clean-cut geometrically pleasing lines of the vehicle. One of the tests I do when a work has been completed is to ask others how they feel. We all have a tendency to love that which is natural and harmonious. Calligraphy has taught me that anything that is harmonious is also beautiful. The crucial usage of harmonic dots to help the calligrapher create beauty is the first lesson a

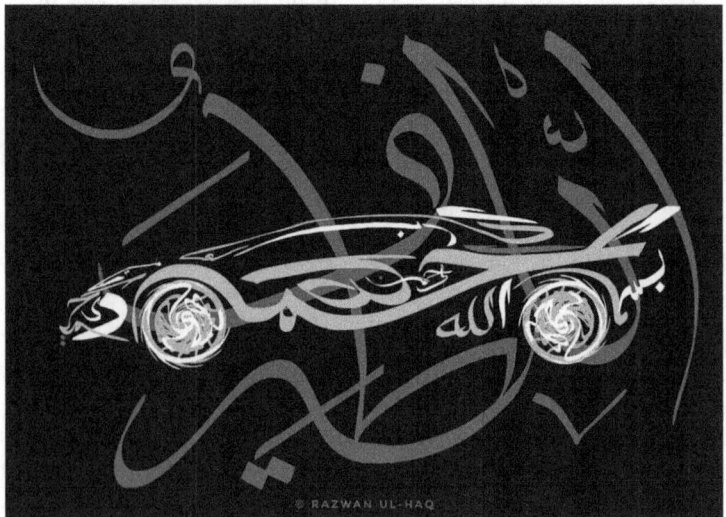

Figure 3.1 The Rave.

Source: Razwan ul-Haq.

calligrapher learns. And our natural propensity to this can be summed up in an oft repeated saying attributed to the Prophetic saying, 'Indeed God is Beautiful and He loves beauty'.

But if we have a natural tendency towards *Husn* (beauty) then what is beautiful? This is a question that has vexed many minds and will continue to do so. I do not believe that beauty is always in the eyes of the beholder – though it is said that only *Majnun* found *Layla* attractive.[9] I think there is a universal beauty which is not always definable – though sometimes we can find ways towards it. I mentioned the harmony of dots earlier, and artists and architects may also use other devices to help them create harmony, hence beauty. I know of painters who still use the harmonies of the *Golden Sector*.

Over the years, I have discovered that calligraphy, if done well, has its own beauty.[10] This is further strengthened by my observation (whilst conducting Arabic calligraphy classes for non-Arabs) that aesthetics of traditional calligraphy stirs hearts of onlookers from different backgrounds.

Whilst on the point of beauty, I feel it is very easy to lose the harmony of the calligraphic form by over-embellishment. It is my understanding that beauty does not require embellishment. It requires harmony. This is where I feel some Muslim architects and artists can create a disharmony. We have all seen examples of where 'Islamic' patterns are wondrous and where they are less so. But I think that there is an added factor. There is an inner harmony in the work of the artist. And this is what attracts me to minimalism.

Art is not divorced from life. Art has a functional as well as a non-functional quality. The inner and outer journey of the Artist is always there, somewhere hidden in the Art. It is no coincidence that in Islam the word *Husn* means good as well as beautiful. To me, it is this goodness that is at once a source for doing something external to the earth and doing something with the earth. The good is within us. When we act, we are to act in harmony, with the good. The good calligrapher is not just one who can copy out letters the best. A good calligrapher has harmony and hence beauty in the self. Too much embellishment in the Calligrapher's own life (whether it be too much food and even too much time spent on Calligraphy, as opposed to looking after family and the poor) can lead to disharmony. I often use the word '*Zuhd*' (asceticism, detachment) to aspiring students of calligraphy to ask them to detach themselves from the outward beauty of the world when we are unravelling its inner beauty and harmony. *Zuhd* is also vital in not being too extravagant in their Art and looking at the most minimal beauty of the calligraphic form in order to fully grasp the nature of its aesthetic. (When I talk of the minimal I do not refer to the minimalism movements in Modern Art.) But too much *Zuhd* can also be ugly, it can create an imbalance in the soul – the beauty of the natural world can act as an anchor to the soul if one understands its temporary nature. It is a journey and not a textbook.

It could be said that *Zuhd* and *Husn* compete for the attention of the Artist. *Zuhd* has a tendency to make the artist veil the beauty of the world, whereas *Husn* points to all that is beautiful in the world. In my own art practice, I feel that *Fitrah* is a criterion that balances the competing demands of *Zuhd* and *Husn*. By seeking to conduct art in tune with nature with all of one's sense – hearing natural sounds, seeing natural beauty, feeling natural beauty and so forth, I feel I am anchored and flowing with the beat of the beauty of creation.

So let us go back to the central question of Islamic Art. In this work, I have suggested that Islamic Art can be a useful term. However, I have also pointed to the problematic usage of the term Islamic Art. I endeavoured to bring a specific delineation to my own artwork. I have briefly introduced the ideas of *Fitrah*, *Husn* and *Zuhd*. Do they help us in defining Islamic Art? My intention is not to create a universal definition. These are my subjective feelings at the current moment in my practice. I do hope that this essay furnishes the reader with how concepts of Islam have made an impact on my art and is a springboard for wider discussion.

Notes

1 Seyyed Hossein Nasr. *Islamic Art and Spirituality*. New York, NY: SUNY Press, 1987.
2 Peter Harrison. *The Territories of Science and Religion*. Chicago: University of Chicago Press, 2015.
3 The feeling is most striking in the *Mezquita* due to the close proximity of spaces – yet one can feel this dichotomy in the different feelings that different religious buildings evoke in almost any other city, from Istanbul to Lahore.
4 Carl G. Jung. *Synchronicity: An Acausal Connecting Principle*. London: Routledge, 1985.
5 Titus Burckhardt. 'The Void in Islamic Art'. *Studies in Comparative Religion*, 4 (2), 1970: http://www.studiesincomparativereligion.com/public/articles/The_Void_in_Islamic_Art-by_Titus_Burckhardt.aspx [accessed 20 July 2022].
6 *Fitrah* could be translated as "primordial nature." The word has been used often throughout Muslim history, going right back to the Prophet Muhammad upon whom be peace. The psychologist Professor Rasjid Skinner once said to me that *Fitrah* is a key, central concept in Islam, and the reason it is not mentioned as a central idea is because humanity was living much closer to nature in the early centuries of Islam.
7 Titus Burckhardt. 'The Void in Islamic Art'. *Studies in Comparative Religion*, 4 (2), 1970: http://www.studiesincomparativereligion.com/public/articles/The_Void_in_Islamic_Art-by_Titus_Burckhardt.aspx [accessed 20 July 2022].

8 *Nastaliq* is an Arabic script that developed in Iran, particularly from the 13th to the 15th century.

9 Writers and poets, particularly of Sufi background have in various placed commented on the ordinary and even "ugly" appearance of *Majnun's* beloved in *Nizami's* (d1209) *Layla Majnun*.

10 A fuller explanation deserves a complete essay. I have begun writing my thoughts about this which I hope to publish in the future.

4 What is Post-*tariqa* Sufism?

Ayesha Khan

Introduction

Sufi expression has transformed since it merged with modern Western social and religious changes. Sufism can be best described using Knysh's definition of 'Islam in miniature', encompassing all the major features of religious tradition, as well as the esoteric and mystical strands of Islam.[1] In the earlier periods, Sufism in Britain was mostly practiced within specific communities and propagated by migrants from the Muslim world, who maintained the Sufi traditions of their places of origin, including their association with Sufi *tariqas*. However, today young British Muslims are exploring Sufism in new and innovative ways. Research on contemporary Sufism has shown how traditional Sufi orders (*tariqa*) are now changing to adapt to a modern global context, with distinctive styles of Sufism emerging since the twenty-first century.[2] This has given rise to multi-*tariqa* Sufi conferences, post-*tariqa* Sufi movements and different individual articulations of Sufi practice and identity.[3] I propose a new way in which to examine the distinct ways young British Muslims are exploring Sufism. This chapter examines how the interaction between transnational Sufism and the wider consumer and sociological environment in Britain has led to new forms of Sufi expression. This can be partly conceptualised as 'post-*tariqa*' Sufism.

Muslim Settlement in Britain

Migration patterns determined the ethnic make-up of British Muslim communities, as pre-existing ethnic and intra-religious divergences shaped early communal organisations. During the late nineteenth and early twentieth century, large numbers of Muslims were travelling to the UK as sojourners because of Britain's colonial relationship with Muslim-majority countries.[4] After the Second World War, primary migration increased as a new influx of people arrived in Britain undertaking unskilled labour.[5] Many arrived due to financial need, educational aspirations and invest-ment opportunities, or were escaping the political upheaval and civil

DOI: 10.4324/9781003330714-7

unrest in their regions.[6] They worked in the UK for economic security, sending money to their families and aspired to return to their homelands. From the 1960s, with changes in immigration laws (1962), many women and children joined their male relatives, which shifted from temporary residence to permanent settlement.[7]

Migrants who became settlers had to find new ways of imagining what community, culture and religion would look like in the future.[8] From the late 1970s, makeshift mosques and Muslim community organisations were created to cater for welfare needs and religious ceremonies, which expanded and became more active in the 1980s.[9] Muslims who had migrated to Britain, from different parts of the world, held diverse ethnic loyalties and intra-religious differences. Consequently, they transferred many of their existing religious understandings and affiliations; communal organisations contained these imprints.

Sufism in Britain

The ethnic and religious loyalties of Muslim migrants were reflected in Sufi practice, which was mostly bound with ethnic identity and association with Sufi orders (*tariqas*). Sufism in Britain was initially practiced within specific communities and propagated by migrants from the Muslim world [10] Mosques, seminaries and Sufi lodges (*khanqahs*) were constructed to gather spiritual guides (*pirs*) and followers of *tariqas,* largely belonging to the Naqshbandi, Qadiri, Chishti and Shadhili orders.[11] This was enabled by globalisation and travel between the UK and Muslim-majority countries, which created international networks to transfer Sufi teachings from the East to the West. Globalisation would also function to create the post-ethnic characteristic of contemporary Sufism by facilitating a network of scholars in Britain, North America and the Muslim world. Predominantly, this began in the 1990s through the 'Traditional Islam' (TI) network, which was promoted to increase religious scholarship in the English language and defend Sufism against the growing influence of Wahhabi and Salafi movements.[12]

Similarly, the Barelvi-Sufi tradition was feared of being abandoned by younger Muslims for an articulate and de-culturalised approach to Islam. The training of Imams in Britain and the knowledge shared by Sufi teachers from diverse backgrounds influenced young Muslims to increase their knowledge of religion and spirituality and re-establish Sufism as a necessary part of mainstream Islam. These Sufi figures communicate their message articulately, in English, emphasising a spirituality which resonates with the experiences of those living in a non-Muslim society. As a result of these changes, contemporary Sufism is much more diverse, transcending ethnic boundaries.[13] Through the Internet and social media, international networks now also extend from the West to the East. There has been a significant increase in communities being exposed to new Sufi *shaykhs, tariqas* and associations, outside of cultural confines.

Research has shown more than half a million Muslim youngsters are under the age of 16 and approximately 55% of the Muslim population are under the age of 25. Although young British Muslims have distinct religious obligations there is also a pull towards a shared national and popular culture.[14] Changes over the last few decades, such as the impact of consumer culture and individualism, continue to affect religious authority and the faith choices made by young British Muslims. This is further influenced by intra-religious transformations, as faith adherents try to adapt to the wider processes of social and religious changes in Britain. Social media and new spiritual organisations have become spaces for young Muslims to negotiate these identities and simultaneously engage in multifarious forms of religious expression and learning.

Neo- and Universal Sufism

Modern-day Sufi expression has been conceptualised through 'neo-Sufism' and 'Universal Sufism', which thus far have contributed towards a better understanding of Sufi expression. The definition of neo-Sufism has varied to account for changes in Sufi practice, such as the participation of Sufis in Islamic reform movements.[15] It has also been used to describe modern Sufi communities, such as British Muslims who engage with Sufism by relating to their experiences of Western culture[16] or groups who use modern technologies to disseminate their teachings and gather followers. Similarly, Universal Sufism is used to label groups which engage with Sufism without Islam. In a more recent study, Jackson introduced this concept through an anecdote about self-declaring 'Sufis' who were not adhering to the demands of the tradition – as he had understood them.[17] He questioned how one could be recognised as a 'Sufi' and whether there is a right or wrong in using this term. How much should one adhere to Islamic tenets to qualify as a 'Sufi' and how can the label 'Sufism' be rightly applied to a group? He also commented on how the Sufi path differs, distinguishing between 'Sufi' and 'Sufism'. My study examines the extent to which these concepts can describe the engagement of young British Muslims with Sufism, as well as the ways in which the concept of 'spirituality' has been adopted interchangeably, and sometimes to substitute the term 'Sufism'.

Post-*tariqa* Spaces

Contemporary Sufi practice has diverged since the early migration of communities that dominated Sufism with strong allegiances to the traditions of the cultural and religious milieu from their places of origin, including their association with Sufi *tariqas*. These transformations were predicted in earlier studies, which considered how traditional Sufi practice would inevitably change when it meets the complex junctions of modernity, in addition to other advances in science, education and social action. The existing scholarly literature on modern Sufi networks has proposed that although formal Sufi orders still exist, there are also 'post-*tariqa*' movements and Sufi practice, absent of a formal *shaykh–mureed* relationship.[18] Post-*tariqas* are associational networks and call for 'collective behaviour and practice rather than individual spiritual training and initiation to a *tariqa*'.[19] These spaces can be both physical and virtual, gathering followers belonging to diverse *tariqas*. They may also allow individuals to engage with a 'Sufi-flavoured' Islam without being formally initiated to any Sufi order or spiritual guide.

Post-*tariqa* spaces can cater to a competitive, fast-paced world, where much of the populace have active lifestyles. There exist a profuse number of options, and different types of gatherings, for people to 'drop-in' and come and go as they please, without any commitment or membership. In addition to this, events may be livestreamed on the Internet, providing people with the opportunity to virtually participate in gatherings and join groups outside of their locality. Post-*tariqa* spaces facilitate spiritual activities, although they may primarily operate as community organisations, creative spaces or charities. Much like earlier regional Sufi groups in Britain, which were exploratory and transnational, they host various types of events and social activities which show voluntary membership, community support and hospitality.[20] These groups allow people to participate in Sufi practice without pledging allegiance (*bay'ah*) to a spiritual guide or order. As these spaces are not limited to hosting spiritual activities, many people happen to join events hosted by these institutions to attend the type of event being held, not due to an interest in Sufism. Such events can range from religious learning, workshops, sport, meditation, poetry and so on. However, most of the events that are promoted events contain a Sufi impetus, connecting attendees to the teachings of saints and spiritual guides, the remembrance of God (*dhikr*) self-reflection (*tazkiya*) and the Prophetic example (*Sunnah*). As no ethnographic research exists on post-*tariqa* Sufism in Britain, I draw on my doctoral ethnographic fieldwork at two different organisations in the North and South of England, both of which are premised on Sufi principles, though not considered *tariqas*. Using methods of participant observation and engaging in informal interviews, I analysed how the spiritual activities in these centres can be conceptualised vis-à-vis post-*tariqa* Sufism. I also researched Sufism in online spaces, by conducting social media research and a netnography of youth *naat khwaani*, young reciters who perform devotional and Sufi poetry on social media. In this context, I also observed the idea of 'Sufi shopping' through the purchase of religious paraphernalia and the consumption of online spirituality. Through qualitative and social media research, I analysed whether post-*tariqa* Sufism exists in the British context and use my findings to help generate its definition. This ethnographic work was carried out at two main organisations, in two different regions in England to help capture the extent of a 'North-South' divide.

Rumi's Cave

Based in London, Rumi's Cave was founded in 2011 by Shaikh Ahmed Babikir, a Sudanese Sufi Shaykh of the Sammaniya *tariqa*. The Cave serves to provide charitable services for local British communities. It was created as a platform through which people could cultivate their personal and spiritual development. They describe themselves as 'an alternative community hub, arts and events venue' and a 'non-defined social space'. Many of their events cater to artistic and creative expression through a lens of spirituality. They host a variety of workshops and courses, whilst also running soup kitchens, exhibitions and poetry events. The manifold events offered at the centre attract different audiences towards Sufi practice.[21]

Rumi's Cave also has an active website in addition to social media pages, with over 9000 on Facebook and over 2000 followers on Instagram.[22] The Friday Sermon (*Jum'ah khutbah*) and the weekly spiritual reminders are occasionally livestreamed on Facebook or uploaded onto YouTube, gathering a national and international audience. Viewers can observe this in real-time or replay the recording at their own convenience. Both managers and volunteers actively engage local communities, irrespective of their ethnic composition and religious leanings, allowing people to share a passion for cultural activities, creativity and learning. Although Rumi's Cave was established by a Sufi Shaykh and was created with the inspiration of the legacy of the Sufi poet Jalaluddin Rumi, they do not call attendees to commit to Sufism by associating with a *tariqa*. Rather, their events implicitly encourage one to connect with Islamic spiritual traditions.

Guidance Hub

Guidance Hub was set up in Manchester in 2016 under the patronage of Shaykh Muhammad Al Yaqoubi, a Syrian Shaykh and member of the Shadhili *tariqa*. They engage youth participation by helping them acquire Islamic knowledge, progress in their careers and partake in the development of their community. Like Rumi's Cave, they are a registered UK charity and their voluntary services exist to serve British communities, despite their cultural and religious background. They also implicitly promote Sufism and relate their teachings and philosophy to Sufi practice without calling for any particular following. Guidance Hub is active online, with a professional website and a following of nearly 8000 on Facebook and over 1000 on Instagram. They encourage a monetary membership, with a monthly fee of 10 pounds. In return, they offer discounts on associated services, including restaurants and cultural clothing, through local business sponsorships.

By operating within major cities, like London and Manchester, participants in both Rumi's Cave and Guidance Hub can find adjacent public transport links a convenient way to access their facilities, which has helped maintain easy access and regular communal visits. Additionally, due to their proximity to local universities and the academic format of some events, they attract undergraduate students and educated classes – this is increasingly common within modern Sufi networks.[23] Unlike leaders of *tariqas*, the *shaykhs* affiliated with these two organisations do not allocate a single deputy to help manage their work with the wider public and instead serve as patrons within these Sufi spaces. They encourage an adherence to the broader traditions of the *Ahl as-Sunnah*, as opposed to following a particular *tariqa*, whilst also inviting those of all and no religious background to their organisations.

Sufism on Social Media

Scholars have previously conveyed how technology has been consumed as a source of religious guidance and spiritual teaching; increasing diversity within the Sufi 'field' and allowing one to connect with such traditions without necessarily observing the traditions of a particular group or sect.[24] Many people appreciate elements of Islamic spirituality or Sufi culture without any formal modes of commitment. The Internet is a significant medium for this type of Sufi manifestation, as it provides one the ability to engage with Sufism through online interactions, by watching or virtually joining gatherings and discussions. Today, social media is a readily available platform for people to engage with and negotiate religion across age, ethnicities, religious denominations and Sufi *tariqas*. Gatherings which were once confined to a private space (e.g. the home) or a single sex (such as male only) are now publicly available to all and can also be livestreamed, therefore observed in real-time. Users can stay updated with the latest events, take spiritual guidance from more than one *shaykh* or *tariqa* and virtually join Sufi groups without the obligation of or feeling bound to any particular *tariqa*.

Sufi Poetry: Youth *Naat Khwaani*

To contribute towards research on contemporary Sufi expression, I observed the online recitation of Sufi poetry through youth *naat khwaani* amongst Barelvi-affiliated Sufis. *Naat khwaans* recite Sufi mystical poetry (*kalaams*) and religious praises (*naats*). *Naat khwaani* amongst young Barelvi Muslims is considered a devotional practice. As 'Islamic music' can be considered a form of paraliturgical worship, *naat* recitation is an oral and aural form of religious and spiritual practice.[25] The diversity of this religious expression is through the recitation of religious poetry in praise of the Prophet Muhammad (*naats*), Sufi mystical poetry (*kalaams*), praise of God (*hamd*) and praise of revered Sufi saints and other religious figures (*manqabat*). *Naat* recitation is commonly held within religious gatherings (*mehfils*), in both private homes and religious institutions.

Through *naat khwaani*, reciters can simultaneously use culturally associated South Asian Sufi practices to relay the teachings of early Muslim saints and teachers in diverse languages, including Urdu, Punjabi, Farsi, Pothwari, Saraiki and Arabic. Today, the youth have made *naat* recitation popular on social media and their large numbers of online followers have allowed them to be perceived as 'celebrities'. Their musical *naat* pieces and professionally produced online videos portray an artistic and creative form of religious expression. However, the reciters do not limit themselves to online performances. Much of their content is indicative of their lifestyles as young British Muslims, which is conveyed through their sartorial choices, status updates commenting on social and religious issues and video blogs ('vlogs') revealing insights into their daily activities.

Although youth *naat khwaani* is increasing in popularity, there remains a fear amongst certain Barelvi Muslims and *ulama* that some of the practices of *naat* reciters are, ironically, causing young Muslims to denounce their loyalty to the Barelvi tradition. Some of these concerns are shared online, via status updates and comment sections, underneath the reciters' uploaded content. These comments share an opinion that some youngsters are choosing to recite *naats* above seeking classical religious knowledge. One reason for this concern is the vast amount of money earnt by celebrity-style *naat* reciters, both during the booking process and through the money given to them during gatherings, which is a customary tradition from South Asia in Sufi musical (*sema*) and *naat* gatherings (*mehfils*). They also claim that *naat khwaans* often 'exaggerate' their recitation in gatherings, arguing *naats* should be recited by displaying respect and humility. To counter this critique, prominent Barelvi *ulama* and renowned *naat khwaans* conduct training and share advice with young British *naat* reciters on how to display the 'correct etiquette' (*adab*) during their recitations.

Over the last 50 years in Britain, *naat khwaani* was popular amongst first- and second-generation South Asian British Muslims in *mehfils* within private homes and religious institutions. However, in recent years, it has become widespread amongst viewers of British Muslim TV shows, such as Noor TV and the Ummah Channel. *Naat khwaani* has also popularised amongst the youth through social media videos on YouTube and

Facebook live. Creative bodies have been established to support this new popularity, such as the National Youth Naat Association (2016) and the Youth Quran Naat Conference (2015). Online video and audio recordings of *naats* are easily accessible for both listeners and reciters, which help in building Sufi networks across national and transnational borders.

Changes in Muslim cultural identities amongst the youth are a key factor in exploring how this contributes to changes in religious experience. Novel forms of Sufi expression, such as poetry and use of the internet, provide new possibilities for a transglobal identity, which transcends Sufi practices confined to a single understanding/group, conveying that traditional *tariqas* are no longer the sole place of Sufi belonging. This can be considered post-*tariqa* Sufi expression. Association to Sufism is voluntary and flexible and is often promoted implicitly, through knowledge, voluntary service and the Prophetic example (*Sunnah*) to help communities revive religious traditions, whilst perfecting their character. This renewal presents Sufism in a way that is contextually relevant. This demonstrates how Muslim youth are replicating a form of Sufism from the past, and to what extent they are finding new ways of promoting Sufism amongst young people , across the divergent *tariqas*.

Sufi *tariqas* sometimes require individuals to limit themselves to initiation with one *shaykh* and/or Sufi order, which reduces their choice of spiritual engagement. However, in post-*tariqa* spaces, individuals are not limited by one mode of religious expression and they can participate in Islam across denominational borders. For scholars in British Muslim studies, this shift shows that where existing Muslim congregations or institutions fail to meet their requirements, young Muslims will create and search for supplementary outlets to the mosque or *tariqa*.

Creative expression has allowed Sufi traditions to become more palatable in the context of religious diversity, where religion must compete and be adaptable in order to remain relevant. These changes raise a number of questions in contemporary Sufi expression, and how it has been acculturated in the British setting. In order to examine these trends, I propose three key research questions: What are the current forms of Sufi expression amongst young British Muslims? What is the role of social media in contemporary religious expression? And what does this new phenomenon tell us about Islam in Britain? I would suggest that this been done through the prism of post-*tariqa* Sufism, and subsequently research could investigate how these new trends have emerged and whether older Sufi *tariqas* are in decline. There is a lacuna in the existing scholarly literature on Sufism in Britain, as cyber and post-*tariqa* Sufi practices. Further research would provide new understandings of changes in religious leadership and authority, as the *shaykhs* take on new roles of presenting spiritual guidance and online figures are perceived as religious influencers.

Notes

1 Alexander D. Knysh. *Sufism: A New History of Islamic Mysticism*. Princeton and Oxford: Princeton University Press, 2017.
2 See, for example, Ron Geaves. 'Transformation and Trends among British Sufis'. In Ron Geaves and Theodore Gabriel (eds.) *Sufism in Britain*. London: Bloomsbury Academic, 2014, pp. 35–52. Sadek Hamid. 'The Rise of the "Traditional Islam" Network(s): Neo-Sufism and British Muslim Youth'. In Ron Geaves and Theodore Gabriel (eds.) *Sufism in Britain*. Bloomsbury Publishing, 2014, pp. 177–196.
3 M. Hermansen. 'South Asian Sufism in America'. In Clinton Bennett and Charles M. Ramsey (eds.) *South Asian Sufis: Devotion, Deviation and Destiny*. London: Bloomsbury, 2012, pp. 247–269. Mark Sedgwick. *Western Sufism: From the Abbasids to the New Age*. Oxford: Oxford University Press, 2016.
4 Humayun Ansari. *The Infidel Within: Muslims in Britain Since 1800*. London: C. Hurst & Co. Publishers, 2004.
5 S. Irudaya Rajan and Aswimi Kumar Nanda. 'Transnational World and Indian Punjab: Contemporary Issues'. In S. Irudaya Rajan, V.J. Varghese and Aswimi Kumar Nanda (eds.) *Migration, Mobility and Multiple Affiliations: Punjabis in a Transnational World*. Cambridge: Cambridge University Press, pp. 1–38.
6 Sophie Gilliat-Ray. *Muslims in Britain: An Introduction*. Cambridge: Cambridge University Press, 2010.
7 Ibid.
8 Pnina Werbner. *Imagined Diasporas among Manchester Muslims: The Public Performance of Pakistani Transnational Identity Politics*. Oxford: James Currey, 2002.
9 Humayun Ansari. *Muslims in Britain*. 2007, pp. 1–41. Available at: http:// mywf.org.uk/uploads/projects/borderlines/Archive/2007/muslimsinbritain.pdf [Accessed: 30 March 2017].
10 Ron Geaves and Theodore Gabriel (eds.). *Sufism in Britain*. London: Bloomsbury Academic, 2014.
11 Ron Geaves. *The Sufis of Britain: An Exploration of Muslim identity*. Cardiff: Cardiff Academic Press, 2000.
12 Sadek Hamid. 'The Rise of the "Traditional Islam" Network(s): Neo-Sufism and British Muslim Youth'. In Ron Geaves and Theodore Gabriel (eds.) *Sufism in Britain*. London: Bloomsbury, 2014, pp. 177–196.
13 Ron Geaves. *The Sufis of Britain: An Exploration of Muslim identity*. Cardiff: Cardiff Academic Press, 2000.
14 Philip Lewis. *Young, British and Muslim*. London: Continuum International Publishing Group, 2007.
15 Martin Van Bruinessen and Julia Day Howell (eds.). *Sufism and the 'Modern' in Islam*. London: I.B. Tauris, 2007.
16 Ron Geaves. 'Transformation and Trends among British Sufis'. In Ron Geaves and Theodore Gabriel (eds.) *Sufism in Britain*. London: Bloomsbury, 2014, pp. 35–52.
17 Roy Jackson. 'Universal Sufis in the UK: Sufism for Everyone'. In Ron Geaves and Theodore Gabriel (eds.) *Sufism in Britain*. London: Bloomsbury, 2014, pp. 53–72.
18 Mark Sedgwick. *Western Sufism: From the Abbasids to the New Age*. Oxford: Oxford University Press, 2016.

19 Marcia Hermansen. South Asian Sufism in America. In Clinton Bennett and Charles M. Ramsey (eds.) *South Asian Sufis: Devotion, Deviation and Destiny.* London: Bloomsbury, 2012, pp. 247–269.

20 Pnina Werbner. 'Playing with Numbers: Sufi Calculations of a Perfect Divine Universe in Manchester'. In Ron Geaves, Markus Dressler and Gritt Klinkhammer (eds.) *Sufis in Western Society: Global Networking and Locality.* London: Routledge, 2009, pp. 113–129.

21 Julianne Hazen. 2014. 'Conversion Narratives among the Alami and Rifa'i Tariqa in Britain'. In Ron Geaves and Theodore Gabriel (eds.) *Sufism in Britain.* London: Bloomsbury Academic, 2014, pp. 137–161.

22 The Rumi's Cave website can be accessed at: https://www.rumis.org [Accessed: 1 August 2018].

23 Martin Van Bruinessen and Julia Day Howell (eds.). *Sufism and the 'Modern' in Islam.* London: I.B. Tauris, 2007.

24 Sariya Cheruvallil-Contractor. 'Online Sufism: Young British Muslims, their Internet "Selves" and Virtual Reality'. In Ron Geaves and Theodore Gabriel (eds.) *Sufism in Britain.* London: Bloomsbury Academic, 2014, pp. 162–175.

25 Carl Morris. 'Music and Materialism: The Emergence of Alternative Muslim Lifestyle cultures in Britain'. In Tim Hutchings and Joanne McKenzie (eds.) *Materiality and the Study of Religion: The Stuff of the Sacred.* London: Routledge, 2017.

5 God and Grime

The Religious Literacy of British Hip-Hop[1]

Abdul-Azim Ahmed

The relationship between religion and music has often been an intimate one. The repertoire of European music remains heavily imbued with religious overtones, ranging from church music[2] to the self-confessed spiritual themes of Richard Wagner's compositions.[3] The relationship is not confined to history either, having been explored in modern music in a recently edited collection by Partridge and Moberg.[4] Hip-hop in particular has been identified as a musical expression with a unique relationship to religion, and Islam in particular. Academic Ebony Utley wrote 'Rap and Religion'[5] about the seeming juxtaposition between references to crime and to God in rap music. 'Scholar-artist-activist' Suad Abdul Khabeer examined 'Muslim Cool'[6] in her book and explored how Islam pervades American hip-hop and expressions of black identity. In the United States, Professor Monica Miller has published a reader[7] as well as an edited collection[8] that taken together present the significant contributions so far, as well as attempting to push the boundaries of existing scholarship. Much of the work presented in Miller and Pinn's 2015 reader considers how religions (Islam, Christianity and Buddhism) operate within and through hip-hop, in lyrics, songs and aesthetics. Contrasting with this however is the edited collection[9] which begins to consider hip-hop as a religion, in terms of its broader wrestling with perennial questions, ontology, meaning-making and communal expression.

Regarding British hip-hop and religion, there have been fewer scholarly endeavours, in part a reflection of the relative youth of genre itself. In this chapter, I present a discussion of the British Grime scene and argue that it reflects the lived reality for both artists and listeners, a lived reality in which religion and religions are central and ubiquitous. I look also to the cross-Atlantic duo Swet Shop Boys, a hip-hop collaboration in which, like Grime, religion and religions are ever-present, but who are drawing on the experiences of a predominantly brown South Asian diaspora. Throughout I argue that to appreciate the music requires an understanding and literacy in religion, an understanding and literacy which is present in the audiences of British hip-hop. The significance of such a study is that it advances our understanding

DOI: 10.4324/9781003330714-8

not only of contemporary religion (as expressed via British hip-hop) but also for the nature of religious literacy itself.

Garage, Grime and Rap

Grime is Britain's most distinctive contribution to the genre of hip-hop. It might sound like rap, but its roots are different. When I was a teenager, I would listen to the local pirate radio station Garage FM. Garage music was heavy with bass, fast paced, with emceeing that was practically incomprehensible over the fuzzy reception. It's from garage music that grime emerges most strongly. The music is usually electronic, produced by talented artists on a laptop and keyboard with incredible musical aptitude, often homemade (hence 'garage'). The lyrics are aggressive and punchy and intimately tied to life in Britain.

Unlike American hip-hop, sociologist Lee Barron contends grime is less focused on 'structural issues' and more on the 'everyday'.[10] Hip-hop is concerned with spaces of the city, the 'ghetto', the 'hood' and the 'projects'. Grime maintained this, speaking of London postcodes and the imagined boundaries of estates and London tube stations. Barron argues while hip-hop slipped into celebrations of 'ghetto fabulous' wealth, grime opted to focus on the mundane (for example, consider Kano's 'Drinking in the West End' or Skepta's 'That's Not Me', both of which celebrate ordinary experiences).

The songs and lyrics are accounts of 'lived experiences' says Barron, 'Wiley's "Bow E3" invokes the council estate he came from, itemizing the various streets which comprise the urban zone'. The sum of it all is that 'Grime, from an ethnographic perspective, offers a holistic social, ethnic, and gendered perception on British culture'.[11] If grime is an insight into culture, postcode identity, and the everyday of East London life, what does it tell us about religion in modern Britain?

The Church and the Road

In this chapter, I put forward two key contentions regarding British Grime music, first, that religion matters to these artists. Second, grime rappers and their audience are highly religiously literate. The argument that religion matters is seen more clearly in Stormzy's debut album – '*Gang Signs and Prayer*' released in early 2017. The album cover evokes the Last Supper by Leonardo Da Vinci, with Stormzy and nondescript associates, all dressed in black and everyone but the artist wearing a balaclava, arranged around the table. The album cover prompted BBC Newsbeat to ask art historian Professor Khadija von Zinnenburg to analyse the image.[12] She stated that:

'I really like this complete immersion in the black studio – the sitelessness or the locationlessness of it', she says. 'To draw it into a photographic studio has something very cinematic and high-tech about it, rather than the much more documentary-type things that he's done in the past, that are much more roving around his neighbourhood'.

Here, she says, 'he's elevating himself into high art'. The obvious comparison isn't missed either, 'he's obviously thinking of himself as Jesus Christ' she adds. Listeners to the album might disagree however. The idea of comparison to Jesus Christ has shadows of Kanye West's lyricism (perhaps most overly in '*I Am A God*') but the message of Stomzy's album suggests something different. The image communicates the central theme of his album – the sometimes-violent sometimes-grim life in urban London, and the religious meaning that pervades it.

'Gang Signs and Prayer' became the first grime album to rank #1 in the charts in the UK, making Stormzy the most successful grime artist yet. His album is experimental, with RnB beats and throwbacks to gospel music, particularly in *Blinded By Your Grace* parts 1 and 2. The lyrics throughout are intense, oscillating from aggressive to vulnerable, mentioning Stormzy's battle with depression, his pride at providing for his mother, and perhaps more than anything, his intense faith in God. The Archbishop of Canterbury and head of the worldwide Anglican Communion, Justin Welby, name-dropped Stormzy's music in the build up to the Royal Wedding in 2018, telling an interviewer that listening to *Blinded By Your Grace, Pt 2* helped calm him for big events. 'There's a line in that, "I stay prayed up and get the job done", I think that sort of sums it up',[13] the Archbishop said. Stormzy, the Archbishop and 'Gang Signs and Prayer' represent a visible moment in which religion and British hip-hop intersected. Part of this is Stormzy's own very powerful and deeply held religious commitments, a commitment he shares with other Grime artists. The recurring message in his debut album demonstrates something found consistently across grime music – religion is a part of life, perhaps the most important. The significance of this is only pronounced when you step back and compare it with 'mainstream' society and its view of religion. People identify less with religion, according to the 2011 census.[14] Almost three out of five Britons feel religion is the cause of more evil than good according to a YouGov poll.[15]

Grime artists commitment and identification with religion bucks the trend of growing 'no religion' which Professor Linda Woodhead describes as 'the new cultural norm'.[16] The national picture hides the fact that believers and non-believers are not equally distributed across Britain. Wales is the least religious part of the UK according to the 2011s UK census, whereas London is the most religious. When I spoke to Stephen Timms, MP for Newham[17] (Ahmed 2016), he was clear, London is a global city of faith. 'Church attendance is rising in London, the Church of England is building its first new church building in London since the 1950s, and on top of that, we have very large mosques, temples, one just opened in my constituency last month'. Newham in East London isn't far from the heartlands of grime music.

Noteworthy too is that this expression of religion is also one that emerges out of Black Pentecostal churches in Britain, churches that have not experienced the challenge of dwindling congregations that currently faces Anglican and Catholic churches in Britain.[18] Pentecostalism in particular has become a resurgent and vibrant part of global Christianity,[19] and this is true of Britain also, especially London.[20]

In the next section, I try to demonstrate that the lyrical content of grime music conveys how grime artists and their audience approach religion not as a forgotten relic of the past, but as a visceral part of their life.

Religious Literacy

In recent years, the term 'religious literacy' has entered popular discourse. Harvard University launched an online course on 'religious literacy'. The Bishop of Norwich suggested that the BBC dropping 'Songs of Praise' was 'another nail in the coffin of our religious literacy as a nation'.[21] The Home Office has been accused of a 'lack of religious literacy',[22] and the former Head of Religion at the BBC bemoaned a 'chronic lack of religious literacy' in Britain.[23]

In terms of defining religious literacy, there are a number of articulations available. In the United States, there is the work of the Founding Director of the Religious Literacy Project Professor Diane Moore[24] and Stephen Prothero.[25] Whereas in the UK, there are publications by Dinham et al.[26] and the working definition of the All-Party Parliamentary Group for Religious Literacy in the Media.[27] All definitions operate around four key areas. The first is understanding concepts of religion in operation, this reflects Woodhead's[28] call for greater reflexivity amongst academics on how they use the term 'religion'. The second can be called comprehension, this relates to the more surface-level but nonetheless important knowledge of specific religions and their history, rituals, festivals, terminology and so on. The third aspect of the definitions above is about being able to communicate religious ideas by drawing on the relevant terms and concepts, and finally, there is an emphasis on contextualisation, being able to draw on the previous three in order to make meaningful and appropriate decisions about everyday life.

So while Songs of Praise is no doubt a valued part of British broadcasting for some, it doesn't really serve as an example of religious literacy – it's not just that it is only Christian, but that it is a very particular expression of Christianity – of Anglican hymns and rural churches.

The Bishop of Norwich's aforementioned fears that the loss of the show was a loss to religious literacy doesn't reflect the full breadth and diversity of what it means to be religious, and have religious literacy, in Britain today.

Shutdown is among the classic grime hits, while it only peaked at number 39 in the charts, it has 56 million views on YouTube and significant radio airplay for such an underground hit. It never went as mainstream as Stormzy's 'Shut Up', but it was nonetheless one of the biggest grime tracks of 2015. To understand the lyrics, the listener needs to be familiar with a) Muslim dietary habits, b) Rastafarianism in general and in particular its sexual ethics, c) the significance of red, gold and green in Rastafarianism semiotics, d) the phrase 'you're not on your *deen*'. *Deen* is the Arabic word for religion, and being 'on your *deen*' or 'on the *deen*' is Anglophone Islamic phrase for religious commitment. Skepta adopts an Islamic conception of religion via the use of the word *deen* as it is a much broader word than the English 'religion'. To accuse someone of not being on their *deen* is to accuse them of hypocrisy and a lack of integrity, not a lack of religiosity. Skepta is not Muslim, and his use of the phrase so casually and comfortably however tells us something important – the religious literacy of both the artist as well as his audience. There is more packed into that one verse by Skepta than the average British Religious Education class.

'Shutdown' isn't an exception either. Krept and Konan's soundtrack contribution to the 2016 film and cult hit Brotherhood is a song titled '*Dunya*', an Arabic-Islamic term, this time referring to the physical world or life, contrasted with the hereafter or paradise. Several artists, including Ghetts, use the phrase '*wallahi*' in their lyrics, a phrase used by Muslims meaning 'I swear to God'. It's often used in Grime to emphasise the honesty and confidence of a statement, regardless of whether or not the speaker is a Muslim. Desperado raps on the group track *Paradise* of life and *haram*, Lady Leshurrs' Queen's Speech 4 offers a wordplay on Ramadan.

The bottom line is clear: if you're a fan of grime, you need to be familiar with a diverse religious vocabulary, drawn from Islam as much as the Bible. Turning back to Lee Barron's argument, if grime is a form of ethnography, mapping the urban landscape spatially and culturally, then the urban landscape is religious and diverse – and your average East London teenager will likely be more religiously literate than his equivalent in Oxford or Swansea. This literacy doesn't emerge out of the religious education syllabus or formal education, but rather the encounters and experiences of everyday life.

It is a reminder that calls for religious literacy, though important, sometimes come from a middle-class elite whose complaints reflect their own monocultural environments which are increasingly becoming secular. When we consider that former Prime Minister David Cameron called for

Muslims to integrate into Britain,[29] and a government-commissioned report by Louise Casey suggested Muslims have yet to become part of the British fabric of life,[30] it is important to recognise that they are failing to account for the experiences and realities of many who live in the UK – in the world of grime, Islam *is* a part of everyday life.

But the presence of the language of Islam in British hip-hop is more profound than simply literacy or knowledge. It is not just that grime artists are familiar with a vocabulary of Muslims, but that they are using Islamic concepts as a means by which to express meaning. In this vein, the language of British hip-hop can be rooted in Ahmed's concept of Islam[31] and his contention of the importance of meaning-making in relation to foundational texts. By adopting Islamic notions of the world (*'dunya'*), honesty (*'wallahi'*) and integrity ('on your *deen'*), artists are incorporating the cosmic and transcendental elements of Islam into their own worldview. Ahmed observes how the practice of Sikh wrestlers in Punjab using the battle cry 'Ya Ali' reveals how they are 'meaning-making in terms of Islam'.[32] This is not 'syncretism' he argues, but 'an act of making things cohere, that is, of making things meaningful together on the same terms'.[33] Extending this logic, grime artists are not adopting vocabulary strange and alien to them. Rather, they inhabit the same world as their Muslim counter-parts, they are able to communicate on the same terms as live within the same paradigm. The proximity of Islam to the everyday life of Grime artists is demonstrated in Wiley's hit *50/50*, referencing conversion and the Muslim faith of 'Ibby and Shifty' (two Muslim members of the Grime collective Roll Deep Crew). Unlike in certain spaces, where converts (usually white) are considered to be race or cultural traitors,[34] there is no such implication if Wiley decided to "turn Muslim", rather there is an implication of continuity. If Wiley was Muslim, he would still operate within the same networks of Grime artists.

It's worth asking the question though – is this religious literacy restricted to Grime? Does British hip-hop in general have anything to offer? *Cashmere*, an album by the Swet Shop Boys, provides a partial answer. The Swet Shop Boys, a hip-hop group consisting of US rapper Heems, British producer Redinho and the multi-talented Riz Ahmed (of Star Wars: Rogue One fame: see the Introduction in this collection). Riz Ahmed has a history of producing music that spoke of his experiences as a British Muslim. His single 'Post 9/11 Blues' re-counted the increasing suspicion faced by Muslims, but also his own success. Swet Shop Boy's 2016 album *Cashmere* takes this same tone throughout. *Shottin* is about a prison convert to Islam, who faces more scrutiny from the authorities as a Muslim than as a drug dealer. *T5* is about ubiquitous airport security checks, and *Zain Malik* is about the cultural appropriation of South Asian identity. Much like

Grime, the lyrics are peppered and layered with religious metaphors and terminology, in this case, drawn from a Muslim and Hindu context of South Asia. In *Din-E-iLahi* ('the religion of God'), Riz MC and Heems both express their relationship to religion. The title of the song is a reference to Mughal Emperor Jalaluddin Muhammad Akbar's debated religious movement.

While Grime is speaking about a black expression of religion, one which includes Islam, Christianity and Rastafarianism. Swet Shop Boys draw on a South Asian expression, combining experiences of Islam and Hinduism. The literacy of the audience is once against at the forefront, listeners of the Swet Shop Boys music would need a familiarity with Islam and Hinduism, of *qawwali* music and the history of the Mughal Empire. Black British and Black American hip-hop influences are present too. The rich historical, religious and cultural melting pot of the album *Cashmere* is aimed at diasporic South Asian audiences, whose experiences of migration, religion and music prepare them to engage with the concepts and terms introduced. What runs throughout the Swet Shop Boys' music is the same expectation of religious literacy in the audience.

Conclusion

Contemporary grime and British hip-hop offer an opportunity to consider what contemporary religious literacy in a context outside of classrooms[35] or policy making.[36] The religious literacy required to comprehend the lyrics of grime music indicate a landscape of diversity and integration necessary to produce the music. Finally, the way in which Anglophone Islamic terms are used by both Muslim and non-Muslim artists indicates how they inhabit the same worlds of meanings, in the terms of expression put forward by Shahab Ahmed.[37] This chapter began with a brief survey of scholarship that considered American hip-hop and religion. I hope this short chapter will encourage other scholars (whether ethnomusicologists, ethnographers or textual academics) to turn to British hip-hop and consider what it can tell us about religion, Islam and everyday life.

Notes

1 Copyrighting and fair-use guidelines prevent direct quotations of lyrics within this article.
2 Gant, Andrew. *O Sing unto the Lord: A History of English Church Music* (Chicago: The University of Chicago Press, 2017).
3 Wagner, Richard. *Religion and Art* (Lincoln: University of Nebraska Press, 1994).

4 Partridge, Christopher and Moberg, Marcus eds., *Bloomsbury Handbook of Religion and Popular Music*, 2019.

5 Utley, Ebony. *Rap and Religion* (CreateSpace Independent Publishing Platform, 2012).

6 Khabeer, Su'ad Abdul. *Muslim Cool: Race, Religion, and Hip Hop in the United States* (New York: New York University Press, 2016).

7 Miller, Monica and Pinn Anthony, eds., *The Hip Hop and Religion Reader*, 1 [edition] (New York: Routledge, 2015).

8 Miller, Monica et al., *Religion in Hip Hop: Mapping the New Terrain in the US*, Bloomsbury Studies in Religion and Popular Music (London, UK; New York, NY: Bloomsbury Academic, 2015).

9 Ibid

10 Barron, Lee. 'The Sound of Street Corner Society: UK Grime Music as Ethnography', *European Journal of Cultural Studies* 16, no. 5 (2013): 531–47, https://doi.org/10.1177/1367549413491937.

11 Ibid, pg 539

12 BBC News, 'Stormzy's Album Cover Looks like a Famous Painting of Jesus Christ - BBC News', accessed 21 June 2022, https://www.bbc.co.uk/news/newsbeat-39076911.

13 BBC News, 'Royal Wedding: Stormzy Song Helps Archbishop with Nerves', *BBC News*, 8 May 2018, sec. Coventry & Warwickshire, https://www.bbc.com/news/uk-england-coventry-warwickshire-44040559.

14 Field, Clive. 'Measuring Religious Affiliation in Great Britain: The 2011 Census in Historical and Methodological Context', *Religion* 44, no. 3 (2014): 357–82, https://doi.org/10.1080/0048721x.2014.903643.

15 Gardiner, Bonnie. *YouGov | Secularism in Britain*, 2018, https://yougov.co.uk/news/2012/03/06/secularism-britain/.

16 Woodhead, Linda. 'The Rise of "no Religion" in Britain: The Emergence of a New Cultural Majority', *Journal of the British Academy* 4 (2016): 245–61.

17 Ahmed, Abdul-Azim. *Stephen Timms MP: Interview on Faith and Politics*, 2016, accessed 15 May 2019, http://www.onreligion.co.uk/stephen-timms-mp-interview-on-faith-and-politics.

18 Kalilombe, Patrick. 'Black Christianity in Britain', *Ethnic and Racial Studies* 20, no. 2 (1997): 306–24, https://doi.org/10.1080/01419870.1997.9993963.

19 Kay, William. *Pentecostalism*, SCM Core Text (London: SCM Press, 2009).

20 Eade, John. 'Excluding and Including the "Other" in the Global City: Religious Mission among Muslim and Catholic Migrants in London', in *The Fundamentalist City?: Religiosity and the Remaking of Urban Space*, ed. Nezar AlSayyad and Mejgan Massoumi (London: Routledge, 2010).

21 Singh, Anita. *BBC Loses Songs of Praise to Independent Production Company*, 2017, https://www.telegraph.co.uk/news/2017/03/10/bbc-loses-songs-praise-independent-production-company.

22 Wilkinson, Laurence. 'The Home Office's Lack of Religious Literacy Beggars Belief', 2019, https://www.thetimes.co.uk/article/the-home-office-s-lack-of-religious-literacy-beggars-belief-358fzwjdr.

23 Burrel, Ian. 'BBC Head of Religion Warns of "chronic Lack of Religious Literacy" in the UK | The Independent', 2016, https://www.independent.co.uk/news/uk/home-news/bbc-head-of-religion-warns-of-chronic-lack-of-religious-literacy-in-the-uk-a6940041.html.

24 Moore, Diane. *Overcoming Religious Illiteracy: A Cultural Studies Approach to the Study of Religion in Secondary Education* (New York: Palgrave Macmillan, 2007), http://public.eblib.com/choice/publicfullrecord.aspx?p=358573.

25 Prothero, Stephen. *Religious Literacy: What Every American Needs to Know--and Doesn't* (New York, NY: HarperOne, 2008).

26 Dinham, Adam, et al. 'Towards a Theory and Practice of Religious Literacy: A Case Study of Religion and Belief Engagement in a UK University', *Religions* 8, no. 12 (December 2017): 276, https://doi.org/10.3390/rel8120276.

27 Khan, Iftikhar. 'APPG on Religious Literacy in Media | Sandford St Martin Trust', 2016, https://sandfordawards.org.uk/all-party-parliamentary-group-on-religious-literacy-in-the-media/.

28 Woodhead, Linda. 'Five Concepts of Religion', *International Review of Sociology* 21, no. 1 (2011): 121–43, https://doi.org/10.1080/03906701.2011.544192.

29 Elliott, Francis and Fisher, Lucy. 'Women Must Integrate, Cameron Tells Muslims', sec. unknown section, accessed 21 June 2022, https://www.thetimes.co.uk/article/women-must-integrate-cameron-tells-muslims-flmnk8c2kqq.

30 Casey, Louise. 'The Casey Review: A Review into Opportunity and Integration' (Ministry of Housing, Communities & Local Government, 2016), https://www.gov.uk/government/publications/the-casey-review-a-review-into-opportunity-and-integration.

31 Ahmed, Shahab. *What Is Islam?*, 1st ed. (Princeton University Press, 2015).

32 Ibid, pg 445.

33 Ibid, pg 451.

34 Franks, Myfanwy. 'Crossing the Borders of Whiteness? White Muslim Women Who Wear the Hijab in Britain Today', *Ethnic and Racial Studies* 23, no. 5 (1 January 2000): 917–29, https://doi.org/10.1080/01419870050110977 and Moosavi, Leon 'The Racialization of Muslim Converts in Britain and Their Experiences of Islamophobia', *Critical Sociology* 41, no. 1 (2015): 41–56, https://doi.org/10.1177/0896920513504601.

35 Jackson, Robert. *Rethinking Religious Education and Plurality Issues in Diversity and Pedagogy*, 2004.

36 Dinham, Adam and Francis, Matthew, *Religious Literacy in Policy and Practice*, 1st ed. (Policy Press, 2015).

37 Ahmed, Shahab. *What Is Islam?*, 1st ed. (Princeton University Press, 2015).

Bibliography

Abdul Khabeer, Suad. 'Su'ad Abdul Khabeer'. *Su'ad Abdul Khabeer*. Accessed 25 June 2019. http://www.suadabdulkhabeer.com/.

Ahmed, Abdul-Azim. *Stephen Timms MP: Interview on Faith and Politics*, 2016. http://www.onreligion.co.uk/stephen-timms-mp-interview-on-faith-and-politics

Ahmed, Riz. 'New @SwetShopBoys Vid AAJA Is Indo-Pak Bolly-Grime Tribute to Qawalli & to Qandeel Baloch(R.I.P.) - RT If u Feel Me: http://www.Swetshopboys.Com/Pic.Twitter.Com/B7lhJlZBSA'. Tweet. *@rizmc* (blog), 6 March 2017. https://twitter.com/rizmc/status/838798790886842368

Ahmed, Shahab. *What is Islam?* 1st ed. New Jersy: Princeton University Press, 2015.

Barron, Lee. 'The Sound of Street Corner Society: UK Grime Music as Ethnography'. *European Journal of Cultural Studies* 16, no. 5 (2013): 531–547. 10.1177/1367549413491937

BBC News. 'Royal Wedding: Stormzy Song Helps Archbishop with Nerves'. *BBC News*, 8 May 2018, sec. Coventry & Warwickshire. https://www.bbc.com/news/uk-england-coventry-warwickshire-44040559

BBC News. 'Stormzy's Album Cover Looks like a Famous Painting of Jesus Christ - BBC News', 2017. https://www.bbc.co.uk/news/newsbeat-39076911

BBC News. *Welby Quells Wedding Nerves with Stormzy*, 2018. https://www.bbc.co.uk/news/uk-england-coventry-warwickshire-44040559

Burrel, Ian. 'BBC Head of Religion Warns of "chronic Lack of Religious Literacy" in the UK | The Independent', 2016. https://www.independent.co.uk/news/uk/home-news/bbc-head-of-religion-warns-of-chronic-lack-of-religious-literacy-in-the-uk-a6940041.html

Casey, Louise. 'The Casey Review: A Review into Opportunity and Integration'. *Ministry of Housing, Communities & Local Government*, 2016. https://www.gov.uk/government/publications/the-casey-review-a-review-into-opportunity-and-integration

Dinham, Adam, and Matthew Francis. *Religious Literacy in Policy and Practice.* 1st ed. New Jersy: Policy Press, 2015.

Dinham, Adam, Matthew Francis, and Martha Shaw. 'Towards a Theory and Practice of Religious Literacy: A Case Study of Religion and Belief Engagement in a UK University'. *Religions* 8, no. 12 (December 2017): 276. 10.3390/rel8120276

Eade, John. 'Excluding and Including the "Other" in the Global City: Religious Mission among Muslim and Catholic Migrants in London'. In *The Fundamentalist City?: Religiosity and the Remaking of Urban Space*, edited by Nezar AlSayyad and Mejgan Massoumi. London: Routledge, 2010.

Field, Clive D. 'Measuring Religious Affiliation in Great Britain: The 2011 Census in Historical and Methodological Context'. *Religion* 44, no. 3 (2014): 357–382. 10.1080/0048721x.2014.903643

Fisher, Francis Elliott and Lucy. 'Women Must Integrate, Cameron Tells Muslims', sec. unknown section. Accessed 21 June 2022. https://www.thetimes.co.uk/article/women-must-integrate-cameron-tells-muslims-flmnk8c2kqq

Franks, Myfanwy. 'Crossing the Borders of Whiteness? White Muslim Women Who Wear the Hijab in Britain Today'. *Ethnic and Racial Studies* 23, no. 5 (1 January 2000): 917–929. 10.1080/01419870050110977

Gant, Andrew. *O Sing unto the Lord: A History of English Church Music.* Chicago: The University of Chicago Press, 2017.

Gardiner, Bonnie. *YouGov|Secularism in Britain*, 2018. https://yougov.co.uk/news/2012/03/06/secularism-britain/

Jackson, Robert. *Rethinking Religious Education and Plurality Issues in Diversity and Pedagogy.* Routledge, 2004.

Kalilombe, Patrick. 'Black Christianity in Britain'. *Ethnic and Racial Studies* 20, no. 2 (1997): 306–324. 10.1080/01419870.1997.9993963

Kay, William K. *Pentecostalism.* SCM Core Text. London: SCM Press, 2009.

Khabeer, Su'ad Abdul. *Muslim Cool: Race, Religion, and Hip Hop in the United States*. New York: New York University Press, 2016.

Khan, Iftikhar. 'APPG on Religious Literacy in Media | Sandford St Martin Trust', 2016. https://sandfordawards.org.uk/all-party-parliamentary-group-on-religious-literacy-in-the-media/

Miller, Monica R., and Anthony B. Pinn, eds. *The Hip Hop and Religion Reader*. 1st ed. New York: Routledge, 2015.

Miller, Monica R., Anthony B. Pinn, and Bun B., eds. *Religion in Hip Hop: Mapping the New Terrain in the US*. Bloomsbury Studies in Religion and Popular Music. London, UK; New York, NY: Bloomsbury Academic, 2015.

Moore, Diane L. *Overcoming Religious Illiteracy: A Cultural Studies Approach to the Study of Religion in Secondary Education*. New York: Palgrave Macmillan, 2007. http://public.eblib.com/choice/publicfullrecord.aspx?p=358573

Moosavi, Leon. 'The Racialization of Muslim Converts in Britain and Their Experiences of Islamophobia'. *Critical Sociology* 41, no. 1 (2015): 41–56. 10.1177/0896920513504601

Partridge, Christopher, and Marcus Moberg, eds. *Bloomsbury Handbook of Religion and Popular Music*. Bloomsbury Academic, 2019.

Prothero, Stephen R. *Religious Literacy: What Every American Needs to Know—and Doesn't*. New York, N.Y.: HarperOne, 2008.

Singh, Anita. *BBC Loses Songs of Praise to Independent Production Company*, 2017. https://www.telegraph.co.uk/news/2017/03/10/bbc-loses-songs-praise-independent-production-company

Utley, Ebony. *Rap and Religion*. CreateSpace Independent Publishing Platform, 2012.

Wagner, Richard. *Religion and Art*. Lincoln: University of Nebraska Press, 1994.

Wilkinson, Laurence. 'The Home Office's Lack of Religious Literacy Beggars Belief', 2019. https://www.thetimes.co.uk/article/the-home-office-s-lack-of-religious-literacy-beggars-belief-358fzwjdr

Woodhead, Linda. 'Five Concepts of Religion'. *International Review of Sociology* 21, no. 1 (2011): 121–143. 10.1080/03906701.2011.544192

Woodhead, Linda. 'The Rise of "no Religion" in Britain: The Emergence of a New Cultural Majority'. *Journal of the British Academy* 4 (2016): 245–261.

Musicography

Kano (2016). *Drinking in the West End*. London: Parlophone.

Kanye West (2015). *I Am A God*. New York: G.O.O.D Music and Def Jam Records.

Krept and Konan (2016). *Dunya*. London: Black Butter Records.

Lady Leshurr (2015). *Queen's Speech 4*. No Label. Available at https://www.youtube.com/channel/UCecMENbFygVpGpg68jMfTHw

P Money ft Desperado, Ruger, Blacks & Little Dee (2016). *Paradise*. SBTV. Available at https://www.youtube.com/watch?v=_XVIIByZYek&index=44&list=PLrdo78rygjoDiCxKgx3Vk5jZBYypW2LLT&

Riz MC (2006). *Post 9/11 Blues*. London: Battered Records.

Skepta (2015). *Shutdown*. London: Boy Better Know.
Skepta ft. JME (2014). *That's Not Me*. London: Boy Better Know.
Stormzy (2017). *First Things First*. London: Warner.
Stormzy ft. MNEK (2017). *Blinded By Your Grace Pt 2*. London: Warner.
Swet Shop Boys (2016). *Zayn Malik*. New York: Customs.
Swet Shop Boys (2016). *Din-E-iLahi*. New York: Customs.
Swet Shop Boys (2016). *Half Mogul Half Mowgli*. New York: Customs.
Wiley (2007). *50/50*. London: Big Dada.

Part III
The Inclusion of British Muslim Art

6   The Playground for Dangerous Ideas

Muslims and British Theatre

Hassan Mahamdallie

In my one-woman play, *The Crows Plucked Your Sinews*, the central protagonist, Suuban, a young Somali woman, is sitting alone in her south London council house watching the first reports of the assassination of Osama Bin Laden unfold on television. The image of Barack Obama standing behind a podium in the White House fills the screen:

OBAMA: *Good Evening. Tonight, I can report to the American people and to the world, the United States has conducted an operation that killed Osama Bin laden, the leader of Al-Qaeda, and a terrorist who's responsible for the murder of thousands of innocent men, woman and children. Last August, after years of painstaking work by our intelligence community I was briefed on a possible lead to Bin Laden. We had located Bin Laden hiding within a compound deep inside of Pakistan. Today, at my direction, the United States launched a targeted operation against that compound. No Americans were harmed. After a firefight, they killed Osama Bin Laden and took custody of his body.*
            [Switch to crowds outside the White House: 'USA! USA! "USA!']

SUUBAN: *No Americans were harmed. After a firefight, they killed Osama Bin Laden and took custody of his body. I felt sorry for the man. I turned off the telly and went to bed feeling sorry for the man. Imagining his martyr's body laid out someplace – in the custody of the USA. I tell you I felt sorry for the man. I felt nothing when they caught Saddam Hussain down that hole, cowardly evil murdering bastard, but Bin Laden. Miskin. Wallahi. I felt sorry for him.*
            I got up the next morning, feeling down, not wanting to turn on the telly, wanting to avoid all the gloating and arselicking by Cameron. Why should it be that the Americans always get their man? Eventually. Inevitably.[1]

DOI: 10.4324/9781003330714-10

During preparations for the initial tour of the play in 2016, the production team discussed whether or not this passage might see us accused of being terrorist sympathisers or glorifiers. A defensive press statement was prepared, just in case. It read:

> I wrote *The Crows Plucked Your Sinews* because I was concerned that the public space to have honest and fearless debates around the big issues that we are all confronted with – war, terror, identity, religion, culture, who belongs and who doesn't, how the past dominates the present, what we are allowed to say and what we are not– was starting to shrink. Fortunately, theatre remains, however precariously, one of those spaces where we can examine these themes in an imaginative way that challenges our preconceptions and dogmas. To do that, many voices, with different views, which we may be attracted to or repelled by, have to occupy the stage. That is the job of the playwright.

Thankfully, we never had to use the statement. After every performance of the play, I and the female actor playing Suuban would hold an open discussion with the audience. No one criticised the character's response to the death of Bin Laden. In fact, during the last night of the 2017 tour of the play in Bristol, a white working-class man stood up and told us that he was so glad that Suuban had evinced sympathy for Bin Laden and the nature of his demise at the hands of US special forces, because he had, like the character in the play, been extremely troubled by the ex- ecution and the crowing of press and politicians. But he had, until he saw the play, been too afraid to admit these thoughts he had at the time, or to mention or discuss them with anyone.

So, had our fears of being hauled over the coals and put in the 'Bad Muslim' box been unfounded? We had certainly underestimated the thirst of audiences and critics for something more challenging than the usual fare and to be exposed to ideas and views outlawed in the main- stream. We also had the benefit of (deliberately) being an independent production company, untouched by the filtering process of being com- missioned by a big theatre and its risk-adverse management team. Others have not been so fortunate.

In July 2015, for example, *Homegrown*, a play about youth radicali- sation written by Omar El-Khairy and directed by Nadia Latif for the National Youth Theatre (NYT), was abruptly cancelled by the NYT management towards the end of rehearsals. The NYT management initially stated that the play, due to be staged in Camden, north London, after a six-month creative exploration with 115 young people, had been halted because it was not up to scratch and had failed to meet 'all of our aims and the standards we set and our members and audiences have come to expect'.[2]

However, it later emerged via a Freedom of Information request that the NYT artistic director, Paul Roseby, had written to public funding body Arts Council England, expressing concern about what he regarded as the play being 'clearly very one-dimensional in tone and opinion'. He complained the project lacked 'in-depth analysis, balance or debate around extremism and instead ... seems to be exploring where to place the hatred and blame'. He informed the Arts Council that he was 'pulling the show' because 'the creatives have failed to meet repeated requests for a complete chronological script to justify their extremist agenda'.

Alarms bells had begun to ring for Latif and El-Khairy when, in their own words: 'at a production meeting, NYT and stage management mentioned they had had a meeting with Camden Police regarding security and safeguarding. As part of that meeting, which was according to them very positive, Camden Police had asked to see a copy of the script and suggested a number of measures including attending the first three performances, plain clothes officers around the entrance, and a visit from the bomb squad. Nadia [Latif] said she wouldn't allow the police to watch an actual show, but they could attend a rehearsal'.[3]

It is instructive to trace where Latif and El-Khairy and the NYT began to diverge. Roseby had originally told the press at the project's public launch that 'I think it is our duty as a young company to commission new work and tell stories that are on the edge that divide opinion. Perhaps the end result theatrically will also divide opinion – it was ever thus – but I think it is worth the risk because theatre is a very powerful medium to explore those issues that can make people feel uncomfortable'.[4]

The original brief had been to respond to the 2014 Birmingham Trojan Horse affair.[5] This was overtaken when it emerged that three young female Muslim school students (one of whom was Shamima Begum) had left Bethnal Green to join ISIS.[6] El-Khairy and Latif expressed the view to the NYT that they didn't want to merely dramatise that particular event but would take it as a starting point to explore 'the environment and narratives both political and cultural around Islam and extremism in Britain today'. Hence the title *Homegrown*.

It is difficult to escape the conclusion that the NYT wanted the excitement of dabbling in British Muslim narratives, but entirely on Prevent-skewed terms,[7] and when the two skilled Muslim creatives it had hired and the cast of independent-minded young Londoners began to workshop the issues from their viewpoints and experiences, the NYT censoriously pulled the plug. As Latif and El-Khairy later stated: 'Muslims are only ever the object in an endless national conversation around Islam, rarely invited to define their own narratives. *Homegrown* probed, pushed back, and hoped to move representations of Muslims beyond simple caricatures and crude Orientalist fantasies. For trying to do that we feel we were censored'.

It wasn't until March 2017 that the public belatedly got a chance to experience an excerpt of the play performed by some 44 members of the original youth cast and to debate the issues surrounding its cancellation at an event in London's Conway Hall, staged by Latif and El-Khairy with human-rights NGO Index on Censorship.[8] In the discussion that followed (which I was asked to chair), the then artistic director of the Bush theatre, Madani Younis, vehemently argued that Latif, El-Khairy and the young people had indeed been censored, and that 'for all its talk about being radical, liberal and left wing, British theatre is, in fact, predominantly a conservative, middle-class monoculture'.[9]

Class is the common denominator that underpins and intersects with other vectors of inequality, underrepresentation and misrepresentation in the arts. A research report published in April 2018, *Panic! Social Class, Taste and Inequalities in the Creative Industries*,[10] analysed cultural and creative workers' values and attitudes, using data from the British Social Attitudes Survey and the UK Office for National Statistics. It revealed that every art form, apart from Crafts, is dominated by people from upper middle-class origins, with people from working-class backgrounds barely represented. It reported there was a distinct 'cultural class' in the UK that has different tastes from the rest of the population. It operates within closed networks, excluding those who do not share its tastes, values or who come from its social group. This cultural class is also distinct in its attitudes, regarding itself as more 'liberal' in outlook than the rest of society.[11]

The report raised a number of important questions: To what extent are cultural and creative occupations accessible and meritocratic if the demographics of its workforce, their social origins and their networks represent a narrow stratum of society? How can they ever shape a much more representative and diverse cultural sector if their tastes, values and politics reflect the class interests of a small privileged elite?

The *Panic!* report detailed how the profession is getting more, not, less rarefied. It found that 'the proportion of young cultural workers from upper middle-class backgrounds more than doubled between 1981 and 2011 from 15% to 33%. The proportion from working class backgrounds dropped by a third from 22% to 13% over the same period'. In 1981, when I started my training as an actor, there were more young people from working-class families like myself entering creative jobs than those from upper middle-class origins; by 2011 that direction of travel had been reversed; with the children of the middle-class origins now dominating the new cohort entering the profession. The gate had closed and largely remains closed today.

This matters in the context in which I am writing because most (but not all) of Muslims in Britain are from working-class backgrounds. Like their non-Muslim counterparts, they do not control the means of cultural production, and thus inevitably their artistic vision, what they want to say and how and to whom, is forced through the distorting conservative lens of this upper middle creative class. The vast majority of voices from the margins are destined to remain at the margins, with perhaps a handful undergoing the de-fanging process of assimilation as they travel to the respectable centre. Issues, such as the place of Muslims in society, the link between the national and the global, the realities of Islamophobia or why many working-class areas of the county voted for Brexit, either remain unheard or undiscussed, or crudely dismissed or parodied.

This structural class inequality is laid over with, and compounded by, oppressive frameworks of 'legal and cultural assemblages' that cast Muslims as 'potentially dangerous and subject to exceptional treatment'. This generates pressures on Muslims to self-censor that which they place in the public arena, policed by what the Brazilian radical theatre-maker Augusto Boal described as 'the cop in the head'. Furthermore, the UK's counter-terrorist Prevent strategy has deliberately invaded the existential realm to 'invoke a nationalised imagination of pre-criminal space'.[12] The pressure to 'play safe' inevitably curtails freedoms of expression that other artists take for granted (and fiercely defend as a universal right). The outcome of this intersection of this class discrimination and Islamophobic oppression is that everyone may choose to have their theatrical or literary take on Muslims, except perhaps Muslims themselves.

Latif and El-Khairy highlighted this contradiction by contrasting their ordeal with a production staged by the National Theatre in 2016. *Another World: Losing Our Children to Islamic State* dramatised interviews 'with people affected by IS and those involved in the fight against it'. The playwright Gillian Slovo's interviews included US generals, senior police, government advisors and academics 'who know about radicalisation'. Slovo's starting point was to understand 'why such a murderous regime should have appeal with anybody that shares the world with us'.[13] The artistic director of the National Theatre, announcing the production, said he might get 'flak' for putting on the show, but that it was right to take part in a 'national debate'.[14] Latif and El-Khairy wrote that contrasting narratives surrounding their show and the National Theatre production, both of which broadly approached the same material, unfairly 'sets up a battle between brave artists and feared Muslims'.[15]

Why does any of this matter? Because the result is that all the big questions facing us remain unexplored and unanswered in the cultural arena by all but the most mainstream and privileged voices. Symptoms are mistaken for causes, possibilities for change fall away, as we are condemned to a closed loop of artistic production, remote from any connection with society at large, and as the theorist Richard Appignanesi has observed, dominated by a narrow cultural class churning out a 'petrified aesthetic of replication'.[16]

In 1963, the gifted African-American writer and polemicist James Baldwin published a small book of immense reverberating power – and he chose to call it *The Fire Next Time*.[17] In it, Baldwin argued that the fate of Black and White Americans was inextricably entwined, as it had been from the very first days when England established a colony in Jamestown, Virginia, and having run out of white convict labour began to enslave Africans and put them to work on the tobacco plantations.

Out of the deep shadows still cast by the barbarism of the Nazi holocaust on Europe's Jewish people, Baldwin argued that the coupling of 'Europe' and 'Civilisation', as a historical claim to superiority over the other races on the face of the earth, had ended. For him, the only way for the western societies to once more advance humanity was for them to accept themselves as they are – not some invented, ahistorical, ethnically pure nation-state that never was. To do this, they needed to liberate and make visible all those they had made invisible, de-valued, persecuted and oppressed, and by doing so 'bring new life to the Western achievements and transform them'. Baldwin argued that it would not do for those previously exiled from the centres of power to be invited to assimilate into a civilisation destructively locked into its own falsehoods – for after all, as he put it, who wants 'to be integrated into a burning house?' A new house for all had to be built from the ground up.

Baldwin concluded: 'White people cannot, in generality, be taken as models of how to live. Rather, the white man is himself in sore need of new standards, which will release him from his confusion *and place him once again in fruitful communion with the depths of his own being*' [my emphasis]. Baldwin's courage speaks to us still across the years; his determination to go beyond accepted paradigms, to pursue the truth to its furthest boundary, to its uncomfortable conclusions. To lay bare things as they are and might be.

There is much talk of 'the other' and 'othering' – how to reach the other and avoid othering them. How to bring them closer to us – to be more like us. But do they want to be like us? Are they eager to be handed the back-door keys to a house on fire? Indeed, when does a Muslim, an immigrant, a refugee or an LGBT individual stop being the other? You have had Somali migration to Europe since the opening of the Suez Canal. The civil war and accompanying exodus took place three decades ago – yet in the UK and elsewhere, Somalis are still considered a refugee community and treated as though they arrived yesterday. To quote 20th-century African American scholar WEB Du Bois – how long must it be before the oppressed are allowed to 'lay aside the status of a beneficiary and ward' and fully become 'collaborators and participants' in society? What must it take for them to become 'a people, rather than a problem' as Du Bois put it? Carried forward by their own history, not forever swept along in someone else's wake? Art has a role to play in this respect.[18]

I like to call my chosen art form, theatre and the playground of dangerous ideas. It has that spatial dimension and the tangible feel of a citizens' arena. All forms of art, in their specific way, have the ability to act as holding spaces where the outer limits of the truth can be put into play, possibilities pursued and human consequences revealed.

Radical change cannot be imposed from above, by an elite who believe themselves to be possessors of wisdom. Change wells up from the grassroots, it does not descend from on high. Solidarity is generated by all those locked out of power who need to come together in a common purpose to make a change – just as divide and rule is a weapon wielded by the powerful in order to resist that change. Standpoint Theory was developed by North American radical feminist scholars in the 1980s and posits that the social groups we belong to, and whether they are near or far from power, shape what we experience and know, as well as how we understand and articulate the world around us. Where we are dictates what we can see, how far we can see and how clearly. Feminist Standpoint theorists argue that those marginalised through inequalities to the outer edges tend to have a more far-reaching view and comprehensive overview of society, than those closer to the centre of power, who tend to have a closed viewpoint. Insight and knowledge arise from those least valued by society.

Let's put it this way: if you are an undocumented migrant, you are constantly scanning for the authorities, as well as for ways to survive. But if you consider yourself, and are considered by others, as a fine upstanding member of society, enjoying the certainties that go with a good bank balance and a nice job and house, you have no need or incentive to scan the horizon, to look around and about, let alone over your shoulder.

If we apply standpoint theory to culture and the arts – it is artists at the periphery that generate innovation; it is here where diverse elements are driven together, new forms of expression arise, and where profound truths emerge. These artists may be marginalised, but they are not marginal. The new vibrant, culturally valuable ways of doing and seeing may travel to the centre, and be assimilated, or appropriated – but they inevitably start life at the radical edges. We need to open up the imaginative spaces in which artists can create and play, sometimes with dangerous ideas, and to provide fresh creative encounters for new, eager audiences interested in what they have to say and show.

In 2013, Pakistani-American writer Ayad Akhtar won a Pulitzer Prize for his play *Disgraced*, about a successful Manhattan lawyer, Amir Kapoor, who shocks a swanky dinner party when he inadvertently utters a transgressive opinion about 9/11 and is subsequently expelled from the garden of corporate grace. I interviewed Akhtar in London on the occasion of the London premiere of the play.[19] He told me, 'I started to imagine an American, of Muslim origin, whose identity was fissured at the root, a man haunted by contradictions'. Akhtar explained that Amir is 'separated from the old-world ways of his Muslim childhood, has adopted every inflection and attitude required to remake himself into the brilliant American success story that he is'. Until in an unguarded moment, a scintilla of who he was emerges in all its rawness, and he is suddenly in free fall. Akhtar told me: 'One of the things the play is about, inside my mind, is how Muslims exist inside the representation that the West has of them. The play is suggesting, or might be suggesting, that modern Muslim identity is still entirely wrapped up in what the West thinks of the Muslim ummah. It's a cul-de-sac'.

Akhtar's conviction was that the Muslim intellectual community had failed to equip Muslims in the West with a roadmap out of that cul-de-sac. For Akhtar, figures such as Edward Said have, as he phrased it to me, 'walked us to the door, but we have got to go out into the world'. Theatre, the playground of dangerous ideas, has the ability to begin to at least sketch out those routes for Muslims out into the world.

Notes

1 Hassan Mahamdallie. *The Crows Plucked Your Sinews*, 2016. The full script can be downloaded at: www.crowsdrama.com.
2 Matthew Henley. 'Revealed: The Unseen NYT Email that Shut Down Isis Play *Homegrown*'. *The Stage*, 3 Sept 2015: https://www.thestage.co.uk/news/revealed-the-unseen-nyt-email-that-shut-down-isis-play-homegrown [accessed 11 July 2022].
3 Personal communication from Latif and El-Khairy, received by the author via email, 1 August 2015.
4 Hannah Ellis-Petersen. 'Immersive Play in East London School to Explore Motives of Radicalised Youth'. *The Guardian*, 2 June 2015: https://www.theguardian.com/stage/2015/jun/02/east-london-school-play-radicalised-youth-homegrown [accessed 11 July 2022].
5 The Trojan Horse affair exploded in 2014 when an anonymous letter surfaced accusing a group of Muslim school governors in Birmingham of an "extremist" takeover of local state schools. This triggered an aggressive and damaging state intervention. The letter was later shown to have been a fake, and the alleged conspiracy was never proved. For an analysis of the affair see Shamim Miah. *Muslims, Schooling and Security: Trojan Horse, Prevent and Racial Politics*. London: Palgrave, 2017.

6 Shamima Begum was one of three teenagers from east London who left the UK in February 2015 to join the Islamic State in Levant forces in Syria. Four years later, upon the fall of ISIL, she was discovered sheltering in a refugee camp in Northern Syria. Shortly after, the British government announced its intention to strip Begum of her British citizenship.

7 The UK government's "Prevent" strategy, launched in 2003 and expanded in 2007, is ostensibly designed to stop people being drawn into violent extremism. In some iterations, it has involved funding or establishing community organisations, including theatre companies. See Therese O'Toole, Nasar Meer, Daniel Nilsson DeHanas, Stephen H. Jones, and Tariq Modood. 'Governing through Prevent? Regulation and Contested Practice in State–Muslim Engagement'. *Sociology* 50 (1), 2016, pp. 160–77.

8 Index on Censorship in a London-based human rights organisation that "campaigns for and defends free expression worldwide". See the IoC case study for a history of the Homegrown affair: https://www.indexoncensorship.org/2019/05/omar-el-khairy-and-nadia-latif-homegrown/ [accessed 11 July 2022].

9 Lyn Gardner. 'Shut Down but not Silenced: Isis Play *Homegrown* Demands to be Staged'. *The Guardian*, 8 March 2017: https://www.theguardian.com/stage/theatreblog/2017/mar/08/isis-play-homegrown-national-youth-theatre [accessed 11 July 2022]. See also: Omar El-Khairy and Nadia Latif. 'Drama in the Age of Prevent: Why Can't We Move beyond Good Muslim *vs.* Bad Muslim?' *The Guardian*, 13 April 2016 https://www.theguardian.com/stage/2016/apr/13/drama-in-the-age-of-prevent-why-cant-we-move-beyond-good-muslim-v-bad-muslim [accessed 11 July 2022]; and Index on Censorship, 'The Inconvenient Muslim: An Evening to Launch Homegrown' Index on Censorship, 2016: https://www.indexoncensorship.org/2017/02/the-inconvenient-muslim-an-evening-to-launch-homegrown/ [accessed 11 July 2022].

10 Dave O'Brien, Orian Brook, and Mark Taylor. *Panic! Social Class, Taste and Inequalities in the Creative Industries*. London: Create London, 2018: http://createlondon.org/event/panic-paper/ [accessed 11 July 2022].

11 The report, drawing on data from the British Social Attitudes Survey, concludes that those in the UK's creative industries hold to "attitudes that are the most liberal, most pro-welfare and most left wing of any industry". How these values actively express themselves, is, of course, another matter.

12 See Charlotte Heath-Kelly. 'The Geography of Pre-Criminal Space: Epidemiological Imaginations of Radicalisation Risk in the UK Prevent Strategy, 2007–2017'. *Critical Studies on Terrorism* 10 (2), 2017, pp. 297–319.

13 Gillian Slovo, quoted a National Theatre video on the making of *Another World: Losing Our Children to the Islamic State*: https://www.nationaltheatre.org.uk/shows/another-world-losing-our-children-to-islamic-state [accessed 11 July 2022].

14 National Theatre artistic director Rufus Norris quoted in Robert Dex. 'National's New Play Explores Why Young Britons Run Away to Join IS'. *London Evening Standard*, 3 Feb 2016: https://www.standard.co.uk/go/london/theatre/national-s-new-play-tells-story-of-girls-who-ran-away-to-join-is-a3171966.html [accessed 11 July 2022].

15 Omar El-Khairy and Nadia Latif. 'Drama in the Age of Prevent: Why Can't We Move beyond Good Muslim *vs.* Bad Muslim?' *The Guardian*, 13 April 2016 https://www.theguardian.com/stage/2016/apr/13/drama-in-the-age-of-prevent-why-cant-we-move-beyond-good-muslim-v-bad-muslim [accessed 11 July 2022].

16 Richard Appignanesi. 'Postculture'. In Ziauddin Sardar (ed.) *Critical Muslim 29: Futures*, London: Hurst & Co, 2019, p. 85.

17 James Baldwin. *The Fire Next Time*. London: Penguin Books, 1965.

18 W.E.B Du Bois. *The Souls of Black Folk*. London: Penguin Books, 1996.

19 Hassan Mahamdallie. 'Review: Disgraceful Fanatics?' In Ziauddin Sardar (ed.) *Critical Muslim 8: Men in Islam*, London: Hurst & Co, 2013.

7   Arts, Heritage and Islamic Manuscripts

Neelam Hussain

Introduction: Engagement of People of Colour and Muslim Communities with Cultural Collections

There is a long tradition of museums and cultural institutions dedicated to Islamic arts, crafts and heritage being established across the Muslim world: Egypt, Turkey, Iran, India and Pakistan have all long-established such institutions. A number of museums have also been built across the Middle East and the Muslim world over the last two decades, or so: the Islamic Arts Museum Malaysia opened in 1998, the Museum of Islamic Art, Doha opened in 2008, Abu Dhabi Louvre opened to great fanfare in 2017 and a dedicated Islamic art gallery is expected to open in early 2023 within the Salar Jung Museum of Hyderabad to house some 2500 Islamicate works and artefacts. In 2021, Saudi Arabia's Museums Commission announced plans to transform and build new museums across the country as part of the kingdom's 'Vision 2030' reforms plan. This is all evidence that there is a demand for such institutions, either within the populations of Muslim-majority countries or among tourist and ex-patriate communities within those countries.[1]

There are also a significant number of large European and North American collections containing Islamic material displayed in either exclusive Islamic art museums or in permanent galleries within national museums, including the Museum of Islamic Art in Berlin; the British Museum and Victoria and Albert Museum (V&A) in London; Musée du Louvre in Paris; the David Collection in Copenhagen; Benaki Museum in Athens; and the Metropolitan Museum of Art in New York, amongst others. Some of these museums have established new or refurbished galleries, often with the aid of Middle Eastern benefactors: the Jameel Gallery opened in 2006 to display some of the 19,000 items housed by the Victoria and Albert Museum in London; the Musée du Louvre opened a dedicated gallery in 2012 to display some of its 18,000 Islamic art objects; the Aga Khan Museum opened in Toronto in 2014 with a collection of over 1,000 items; and the British Museum opened its

DOI: 10.4324/9781003330714-11

Albukhary Foundation Gallery to re-display the museum's Islamic collection in October 2018.

A number of these collections, including the British Museum and Victoria and Albert Museum, were direct beneficiaries of the spoils of colonialism. Considering the size and substance of many of these collections, and the fact that significant portions of the collections originated from countries from which the UK has a significant diaspora, it would follow that they would actually attract people of colour, minority ethnic and Muslim audiences. With significant publicly funded budgets at their disposal, it is surprising, therefore, that the visitor figures of these national institutions housing such prestigious collections do not reflect visitors from the range of communities whose heritage is represented in the collections. Considering diversity of audiences is something they are required to account for, it is perplexing that they still fail to engage minority groups – even where those 'minority' groups form a significant proportion of the local population. Whilst museum visitor figures are not broken down by faith groups, we do have figures for 'ethnic minorities', with Muslim communities largely falling under this category. The 2002 Public Accounts Committee report highlighted that only 7% of V&A visitors came from ethnic minority backgrounds.

Whilst the figures have improved since, they still make dismal reading with only 17% of visiting UK adults from ethnic minorities in the year 2015–2016.[2] The figures are better for some other London museums that hold significant Islamic collections, though they are still well-below national averages. In the British Museum's 2007 Annual Report, only 15% of visitors from the UK were from ethnic minorities.[3] Bearing in mind ethnic diversity of London's population – a city where almost 40% of the population is from a Black, Asian or minority ethnic background – and the diverse cultures that are represented in the collections within these permanent galleries, it is inexcusable that the figures for London's national public museums are so much lower than the national averages. The figures on diversity trends provided by the 'Taking Part Survey' published by the Department for Culture, Media and Sport showed that, although engagement from under-represented demographic groups has risen over the last ten years, it still continues to be significantly higher for the white ethnic groups.[4] The gaps vary in the statistics looking at arts engagement, heritage engagement, and museums and galleries, but they all show significant disparities compared to white audience figures (8.5%, 18.5% and 9.5%, respectively).

The Relevance of Museums: Decolonisation and Diversity

The statistics presented above beg the questions: What are the reasons for the failure of museums and art galleries in the UK to attract and engage people of colour and Muslim audiences? Does it really matter? Statistics show that museum visitors are mostly older, white and middle class. As such, it is easy for museums to find themselves trapped, consciously or unconsciously, into developing their programmes to suit such an audience and avoid presenting them with anything that may challenge this target audience's expectations, or themselves as institutions. Yet, it is essential that they serve audiences beyond their traditional patrons in order to fulfil what has been described as their 'cultural contract' – or else risk irrelevance to those they seek to attract.[5] The statistics and barriers to engaging more diverse audiences are complex and include race, age, class and socioeconomic status amongst other things. These factors have been well-documented and are routinely noted in the annual reports and surveys referred to earlier. The present focus is on calls in recent years to make cultural institutions more relevant to diverse audiences and holding cultural institutions to account for failing to do so. Recent debates have brought into focus issues around the origins of collections and the context of museums' collecting histories, the lack of ethnic diversity in the teams who make the decisions about programming and in senior leadership positions, the relevance and tone of programmes, and how the (de-)contextualising of objects raises important questions about the overall place and purpose of these institutions in civil society.

In relation to the collections within national public cultural institutions, a major focus of recent calls to hold museums to account in their duty to fulfil their cultural contract and make themselves more relevant to broader society has been the need to have honest conversations about the circumstances under which objects were removed from their place of origin and how the collections were formed. Debates on the repatriation of objects, particularly those that were plundered or taken through coercion or under the shadow of unfair balance of power during the period of British and western European colonisation, have gained wider public attention in recent years. From the Benin Bronzes at the British Museum to Ethiopia's Maqdala treasures at the V&A, there has been an ongoing debate about the housing of such cultural artefacts amongst growing pressures from activists and the governments of the countries from where the objects originated to return them to their homeland. In November 2017, French President Emmanuel Macron announced that the temporary or permanent restitution of African cultural heritage objects to Africa was going to be a 'top priority' for France.[6] A year later, Macron endorsed the Restitution Report he had commissioned, written by Felwine Sarr and Bénédicte Savoy, which recommended the widespread return of cultural artefacts removed from Africa during the colonial era. He agreed to immediately return to Benin 26 artefacts that were seized by General Dodds as the spoils of war in 1892. Both the report and the subsequent announcement marked a milestone in the struggle by African countries to recover objects looted by European colonisers.[7]

Since then, other former colonial powers in Europe have begun to reflect on their position on the issue. The cultural authorities in Germany agreed on a set of guidelines for the return of artefacts in March 2019. A week earlier, the National Museum of World Cultures in the Netherlands promised it would investigate its own collection and presented new rules for reclaiming artefacts looted under Dutch colonial rule.[8] The response from British institutions, however, has been much more tepid. Whilst the British Museum announced in December 2018 that it would temporarily return to Nigeria its collection of Benin Bronzes – looted by British forces during the Benin Expedition of 1897 – under a loan agreement, it has resisted any kind of pressure regarding the statue Hoa Hakananai'a, stolen from Easter Island in 1869, and Greece's calls to return the Parthenon Marbles. The authors of the French report, Sarr and Savoy, have criticised the British Museum for their reluctance to face up to the issue of repatriation of artefacts in its collections. Citing its stance on this issue, the institution's sponsorship from BP, and the treatment of workers, one of the British Museum's trustees, the author Ahdaf Soueif, resigned from her position on the Board in July 2019. She urged for it to take 'a clear, ethical position' on matters of critical concern to those it wishes to engage.[9]

Elsewhere in London, the V&A's director, Tristram Hunt, attempted to engage in the debate with a comment piece titled 'Should museums return their colonial artefacts?', which outlined some of the recent developments across Europe on the restitution of stolen artefacts. He acknowledged the 'less pretty circumstances' under which the Maqdala crown came to be part of the V&A collections but skirted around giving a definitive position on the museum's stance on restitution and repatriation. Instead, Hunt cautions against action being 'dictated by a political timetable' and insisted that there 'remains something essentially valuable about the ability of museums to position objects beyond particular cultural or ethnic identities.'[10] Hunt went further by (erroneously) conflating the legal and ethical issues of restitution and repatriation with growing calls for 'decolonisation' and concluding that, 'For a museum like the V&A, to decolonise is to decontextualize.' His criticism of calls for decolonisation appears to be that the process lacks nuance and that it removes objects from their context. The proponents of decolonisation, however, would strongly disagree with this description: decolonisation aims to *add* context, depth and new knowledge to collections by asking people to re-examine objects and question the way their histories have been presented until now. Hunt's piece reignited much discussion, with some questioning, what is there for museums to be afraid of? Is it their loss of authority or power? Or is it, perhaps, that stories of people and places outside the traditional agreed narratives will be told?[11]

As mentioned earlier, some of the key concerns in discussions around decolonisation include the history and collection practices of institutions, the programming and discourse around exhibitions, and the issue of ethnic diversity of staff and representation. These calls to decolonise cultural institutions are underpinned by critical discourse in post-colonial studies highlighting the ideological, political and economic matrix within which writing about culture takes shape.[12] The work of Edward Said, Gayatri Spivak and Homi Babha in particular have been influential in understanding structures of dominance and how they infiltrate and influence culture.[13] Post-colonial discourses and decolonisation initiatives acknowledge these power structures and strive to pursue different roles and missions in the original context of collections and institutions. They are powerful tools that interrogate historical assumptions about western positions as objective caretakers of the world's cultural legacy. Proponents argue that it is only when institutions acknowledge power structures, whether in terms of how objects came to be owned or the historical and present-day structures, that we have greater accountability to local communities.

Calls for the decolonisation of museums also stem from narratives surrounding people of colour that traditional histories perpetuate, and exasperation at the apparent lack of interest from most institutions to address this issue. Initiatives that seek to challenge existing practices and narratives, such as 'Decolonise This Place' in Brooklyn and Whitney Museums, have emerged on both sides of the Atlantic.[14] They demand that issues of reparation and repatriation are addressed, call for greater diversity in the recruitment of staff and executive leadership and demand that the colonial heritage of buildings and their collections are acknowledged in curatorial practices, programming and exhibitions, as well as improvement in the working conditions of ground staff – things that were also echoed in the Ahdaf Soueif's resignation. Such calls to decolonise institutions have also extended beyond museums and into academia and broader society with campaigns like 'Rhodes Must Fall' at the University of Oxford, which called for the removal from the outside of Oriel College the statue of Cecil Rhodes, the imperialist business magnate who drove the annexation of vast swathes of land in southern Africa. In June 2020, a statue in the city centre of Bristol of the trans-Atlantic slave trader, Edward Colston, was pulled down from its plinth and rolled into the harbour during the global protests against racism and police brutality that were held in the aftermath of the murder of George Floyd. These movements want a radical reassessment of history and to raise awareness of the legacy of colonial processes across present-day institutions, including the way history is taught.[15]

Addressing the lack of diversity within the UK museum sector workforce is something that has been highlighted as a major challenge for museums and art galleries – it was also highlighted in the National Museum Directors Conference, Cultural Diversity Final Report, 2006.[16] Increasing diversity in these workplaces will inevitably affect the power structures of these institutions, and the kinds of decisions that are made on what is worthy of study. There is an acknowledgement, however, that diversity of the workforce alone is not enough to create the more radical changes that are needed to create systemic change. A collective of artists and thinkers in Birmingham initiated a 'Decolonise Not Diversify' programme in October 2016 to explore some of the concerns that a focus on diversity alone ignores the systemic changes that need to be made. These concerns were also raised by the writer Kavita Bhanot in an article about the dangers of 'diversity' becoming a tick-box exercise that makes institutions feel they are doing something without addressing systemic structural biases.[17]

In terms of collections, some institutions have responded to these movements through the way they develop their collections. In Bradford, Cartwright Hall developed a project to build a transcultural collection to reflect changing communities in the city. Manchester Museum is due to open a South Asia gallery and has created a youth-led programme that explores the shared cultures and histories of the UK and South Asia.[18] Other museums have attempted to offer fresh perspectives on their collections through community partnerships and co-curated exhibitions. Birmingham Museum and Art Gallery invited co-curators of colour to develop an exhibition from the museum's permanent collection that addresses its colonial history. 'The Past is Now: Birmingham and the British Empire' exhibition, which opened in December 2017, addressed Birmingham's role within the British Empire and the relevance of these stories today. It was received with much praise. Nevertheless, these projects have not been without their problems: one of the co-curators of the 'The Past is Now' exhibition, writer and researcher Sumaya Kassim, has written about the difficulties of working with institutions, and fear that words like decolonisation could become devoid of agency or a 'pretty curio with no substance', if museums are not really prepared to address the complexity of ideas that underpin the process with self-reflection and a critical eye.[19]

With regard to the specific engagement of Muslim audiences, one of the main challenges is in the way cultural institutions define what is worthy as an exhibition. In terms of content, even where cultural institutions are appearing to consciously acknowledge their colonial legacies and present a desire to move away from traditional attitudes about the way to educate people, there is still a reluctance to fully embrace the process in terms of the content of exhibitions. As someone who works in the sector, I have come across protests from colleagues in the heritage sector that Muslim communities are resistant to engagement or are only interested within a narrow remit of topics, such as the Quran or calligraphy. These complaints include a paternalistic and patronising perception – on the part of heritage practitioners – of what is considered innovative or worthy of exhibition and the view that it is the Muslim communities they have worked with who are resistant to engage or are uninterested in arts outside what may be considered traditional 'religious' or orthodox boundaries. There may well be some element of truth to this for *some* Muslims who don't ordinarily engage with arts and cultural programming. Nevertheless, such attitudes overlook the fact that there have been a range of exhibitions across the UK, both contemporary and traditional, that ventured further afield and have been very successful at engaging Muslim audiences: exhibitions about the journey of the annual Hajj pilgrimage, calligraphy, geometry, epic works of literature and poetry, architecture (past and present), the partition of India and Pakistan, Islamic and South Asian textiles, Sufi music, and the lives of early immigrants to Europe. The common factor to all of these exhibitions is that they invited a strong emotional response from their prospective audiences.

The Mingana Collection of Middle Eastern Manuscripts

The remainder of this chapter will consider some of the opportunities and challenges of engagement projects with the Mingana Collection at Cadbury Research Library (CRL) in light of some of the issues raised above about collections, programming and diversity. The manuscripts in the Mingana Collection were acquired during the 1920s and 1930s by Alphonse Mingana (1878–1937). The collection includes over 2000 Arabic and Persian manuscripts, as well as a selection of paintings and coins from the Muslim world. The contents of the collection range from religious and scientific, to literary and poetical texts with paintings and illumination. It provides a unique and rich resource for both academic research and exploration of religious and intellectual history as well as the cultural and artistic heritage from the birth of Islam up to the early twentieth century. A number of the Mingana manuscripts are lavishly illuminated with elaborate designs, gilding to the title pages, frontispieces and headpieces, and/or contain paintings and illustrations. All of this provides a lot of scope for work on the art and material culture of the Islamic world that would appeal to a broad spectrum of people across age groups; not only to those with a specialist interest in manuscripts but also to school children, students, local communities or the simply curious. As such, the CRL has a responsibility to share this important collection as widely as possible. The rest of this chapter will discuss some of the considerations of widening access to the Islamic collections both as a research library and as part of a public engagement programme with reference to some of the broader debates and discussions about the purpose and place of cultural collections.

Scholarship and Accessibility

As a research library, one of CRL's primary functions is to facilitate research and scholarly engagement with the collection. Curators and archivists actively encourage students to explore the collections, running sessions as part of undergraduate and post-graduate programmes to facilitate this. Access to CRL's reading room is also open to the public upon (free) registration. We also work with secondary school groups and the university's outreach teams. Although the university location does provide teaching and research opportunities, it also creates some challenges. A research library can be intimidating to prospective members, particularly the general public, as items are not available off-the-shelf as in traditional libraries. Whilst the publicity about the Birmingham Quran Manuscript has created a stream of enquiries about the collection from members of the public, it is difficult to quantify the number of potential readers whose access is hindered due to issues around the accessibility of a campus-based research library.

For visitors outside academia, the location of a research library on a university campus can often be intimidating or geographically inconvenient. It is well-documented that universities are often perceived as exclusive institutions that are remote from the communities in which they are situated. This will remain an obstacle without some radical thinking on the part of the universities. Partnerships with community organisations and hosting community events, such as the Green Heart Festival that was re-introduced by the University of Birmingham in 2019, will go some way towards opening up the campus to the public but continued and greater efforts are required at an institutional level.

The 'Birmingham Quran Manuscript' and Engagement with Muslim Communities

The Mingana Collection has just as much, if not more, significance to people outside of academia whose faith and cultural heritage are represented in its contents. The CRL has developed and delivered various public engagement projects at a local, national and international level, to increase awareness of the collection and widen access to it. Since the dating of the Birmingham Quran Manuscript, the CRL has developed and led a programme of activities and public engagement projects at a local, national and international level. In 2016, a community friendship group for South Asian women, DOSTI, run by the 'Go Women! Alliance (GOAL)', took part in a project run by the collection's development officer Josefine Frank, and artist Shaheen Kasmani, exploring Islamic paper-making and binding techniques. The group was supported to produce Islamic-style marbled paper and bindings inspired by the collection.[20] Their work was later displayed at the university, and they were invited to see the displayed items. Several of the women involved spoke little or no English and had not visited a museum or university before and commented on how much they had enjoyed the project and working in such a space. They also expressed gratitude for the opportunity to see such rare manuscripts and artworks, particularly Quran manuscripts and books and paintings from the Indian subcontinent. They expressed a pride and connection with the items and wanted to share their experience with their families and friends. Several commented on how the collection reflected a part of their heritage that they would like to share with the younger generations of their own family. In 2017, local primary school groups were invited by our education consultant to work with a local artist and collaborate to produce their own manuscript inspired by the Mingana Collection. CRL has also hosted and supported visits from local, national and international groups to engage with the collection. In addition to these projects, CRL delivers workshops, handlings sessions allowing closer inspections of the material and hosts school visits and tours of the facilities for school groups throughout the year.

These projects have drawn on some of the many benefits of the university campus location of CRL, such as facilities to accommodate visiting groups on campus and to support teaching, its location at the heart of the Edgbaston campus, accessibility of buildings, support and engagement with various departments across the university, and the opportunity to be part of the wider programme of cultural activities delivered at the university. Another benefit of being part of a large and busy campus is the opportunity to engage a wide student body of over 35,000 students with the collection, through exhibitions. CRL has a busy exhibition programme at various sites on campus, including the atrium of the university's new library. The most recent exhibitions focused on manuscripts and works of art with Indian origins: *Mughal Miniatures: Power, Piety and Poetry*, and *The Mughals: Power and Beauty at the Indian Court* displayed at the Barber Institute of Fine Arts.[21] The exhibitions proved popular with students, staff, external visitors and school groups and attracted people of colour who commented that they do not ordinarily visit the Barber Institute. The exhibition was accompanied by talks and art workshops engaging local communities. Visitors have enjoyed the opportunity to witness and find out more about items from the Mughal imperial library, a page from the personal album of Emperor Shah Jahan and the manuscripts of famous authors and their works.

The so-called 'Birmingham Quran Manuscript' has been the source of much public attention in recent years after the results of radiocarbon dating of the parchment leaves of this seventh-century Quran manuscript (*Mingana Islamic Arabic 1572a*) demonstrated that it was one of the earliest surviving manuscripts of Quran in the world, with the upper end of the date range (568–645 CE) falling within 13 years after the death of the prophet Muhammed. The announcement was made in July 2015 and became a huge international news story with extensive media coverage.[22] The widespread interest and demand to see the manuscript that ensued resulted in a public exhibition of the manuscript with an explanation of the radiocarbon results, which was held at the University of Birmingham in October 2015. Over the three-week exhibition, the exhibition welcomed 8000 visitors across demographics – individuals, families, academics, community groups and schools – not just locals but from across the UK, Europe, the Middle East, the United States, Pakistan and Malaysia. Although there was a range of people visiting, a majority of the visitors were Muslim; visitors frequently reported that it was the first time they visited an exhibition. Visitors expressed enjoyment, interest and appreciation of the opportunity to view the manuscript. However, what was most evident from visitor engagement and feedback, particularly from Muslim visitors, was pride in their cultural and religious heritage being on display and available to share with the wider society. A deep emotional response to the manuscript was also very evident. This was at a level far beyond what could have been anticipated when news was first released.

The radiocarbon dating of the Quran manuscript has been the cause of much debate and has met with a large, persistent demand from the public to explore and understand its significance. Our most ambitious international engagement project was the Birmingham Quran Manuscript exhibition delivered in Sharjah, Abu Dhabi and Dubai as part of the 2017 UK-UAE Year of Culture. The UAE Ministry of Culture and Knowledge Development and the British Council worked with the University of Birmingham as strategic partners to deliver a series of high-profile exhibitions, school visits and calligraphy workshops. The team that designed and delivered the various elements of the project was a mixture of professional staff and academic staff, including those with expertise in the curation of exhibitions, conservation, learning programmes and research. In conjunction with the Quran exhibitions and in order to meet this demand for as broad an audience as possible, CRL developed a four-week Massive Open Online Course (MOOC) that detailed the significance of the radiocarbon dating, the manuscript's provenance and its conservation. In response to discussions and feedback at previous exhibitions, the content of the MOOC also covered a description of its characteristics and how they fit into the development of Arabic script and calligraphy and the arts of Quran manuscripts.[23] The MOOC has been presented twice so far (in 2017 and 2018) attracting thousands of learners from around the world. The MOOC has provided the CRL an opportunity to break geographical boundaries and engage with audiences at a global level. The CRL still regularly draws in visitors who would like to see it. However, due to sheer demand and issues of conservation, it is not possible to accommodate the level of requests to see the manuscript. Instead, there is a permanent display of a facsimile copy on parchment in the CRL's reading room, with additional physical and digital exhibitions intermittently held on campus in order to meet the demand as much as possible. There is also a dedicated section on the CRL website with high-resolution images and an explanation of its significance. Statistics on visitors to the website indicate that this section continues to be frequently visited.

As well as the CRL's own exhibition and engagement programme, we have organised and collaborated on a number of exhibitions aimed at the general public that were very successful in engaging people of colour and Muslim audiences in particular. Over the years, CRL has loaned various items to Birmingham Museum and Art Gallery for exhibition. In 2005, a group of manuscripts from the Mingana Collection were loaned as part of their 'Illuminating Faith' exhibition. Fourteen manuscripts were loaned as part of their 'Qalam: The Art of Beautiful Writing' calligraphy exhibition that took place in 2013. This exhibition attracted 33,000 visitors over three months, with 60–70% of them categorised as being from Black, Asian or minority ethnic groups, which was twice the usual audience figures for this category; 20% of these visitors had never visited the museum before.

The Birmingham Quran Manuscript was loaned to the new *Faith in Birmingham* gallery that opened at Birmingham Museum and Art Gallery in early 2016 with the manuscript serving as the main gateway object for Islam. Over the six months that the manuscript was on display at the gallery, they received over 56,000 visitors. The overall number of visitors, and the significantly higher engagement from people of colour and minority ethnic groups, particularly in relation to Muslim audiences, attests not only to the demand to see the manuscript but also to the fact that these audiences do want to engage with museums and cultural institutions more generally. The figures also highlight the fact that there is a significant portion of the city's population who are otherwise not benefitting from engagement with cultural collections even though they are willing to do so. The key to engaging with these groups is for institutions to take on the onus to create relevant programming that speaks to the audiences they seek to attract in a more meaningful way.

The general feedback received over the course of the community engagement projects that the CRL has been involved in that drew high visitor numbers from people of colour and Muslim communities highlights deep emotional responses to the items on display, particularly with regard to the Birmingham Quran. Other public engagement projects, such as the schools and student groups, local community groups and even visits from academic groups, have drawn positive responses with Muslim visitors leaving with a great sense of pride in a collection that reflects their heritage. Whilst it is not realistic to expect to replicate the same level of interest with other objects as there has been with the Birmingham Quran Manuscript – where the level of interest for many of the Muslim visitors was due to the significance of the early dating – there are still lessons to be learned about the strong desire amongst Muslim communities to explore cultural and religious heritage: the spiritual, emotional and cultural connections to objects are just as important as any academic debates about the significance of a group of manuscripts.

Engagement work will also inevitably raise questions about the provenance of collections; an issue that requires frank discussions. Although the Mingana Collection is not a direct beneficiary of colonialism in the way many of other major British and European collections are, the context and power structures of how these objects were purchased or otherwise displaced from their places of origin before they arrived in the UK is still an important contextual element that is addressed frankly in our work with the collection. This is something we actively address at all levels during teaching sessions, whether it is with external visiting school groups, university students or members of the public. Our work has also seen some unexpected responses. I have regularly received enquiries from Muslim and people of colour participants through our outreach work about entry routes into curatorial or heritage work; enquiries from people who had never previously considered it as a career. On the other hand, non-Muslim participants have reported that exploring the Mingana Collection has challenged some of their preconceptions of what other cultures have contributed and achieved.

One of the positive outcomes from discussions with artists and heritage practitioners at the MBRN Islamic Arts and Heritage (2017) conference held at the University of Birmingham was that there would be much interest and potential for the Mingana Collection to be an integral part of a national framework of heritage activities if facilities and funding could be secured. Although CRL has had an active engagement programme in place, there is still, however, a lot of unexplored potential with the collection and considerations that require attention in order for us to reach out even more – considerations that also apply to other institutions. Exhibitions and engagement programmes need to take into account and more actively cater for the interests of their potential

audiences from the outset in terms of the design of their cultural programmes: not as an afterthought when trying to find ways to engage
more people. Programming that focuses on both cultural and faith traditions brings in audiences that might not otherwise be interested.
Diversity of the workforce is another essential component to driving in
some of these changes and offering fresh perspectives about what might
work. Institutions must reflect the range of audiences with whom they
would like to engage in the make-up of their teams across all levels.
Furthermore, they need to appreciate the added value that a diverse
workforce brings: academic expertise combined with lived experiences,
potential connections and the ability to communicate with local communities too. Some of CRL's more recent engagement work with the
Birmingham Quran Manuscript and the Mughal material was certainly
informed through a mixture of some of these elements. To summarise
what has worked best with our engagement projects: it is the design of
programming around objects from the collection to which audiences can
connect, through the stories these objects tell, and the work of a team
with a mixture of professional and academic members that includes the
unique perspectives and insights of staff from minority backgrounds.

Future Directions for Muslim Engagement in the Arts and Cultural Sector

The engagement and participation figures for the projects that the CRL
has been associated with stand in contrast to the statistics for people of
colour and minority ethnic groups earlier in the chapter. They demonstrate that Muslim communities *are* actually willing to engage if the
subject is meaningful or educational to them. They also reflect the fact
that engagement and visitor figures for ethnic minorities might have less
to do with ingrained attitudes towards cultural institutions and more to
do with failures on the part of institutions to make content relevant to
the interests of the communities they wish to engage. Exhibition content
and programming are key to attracting new audiences from under-
represented groups who might be seeking content that stirs emotional as
well as intellectual responses. Diverse workforces and honesty about
collection histories also play an important role in making museums
relevant to new audiences. Another thing to consider is satellite projects
that take exhibitions and events into local communities: on their local
high streets; in the areas where higher concentrations of Muslims and
people of colour live, and shop, and where there is a high footfall. Many
of the areas that are densely populated with communities of colour
also boast some of the highest proportions of independent retailers,
attracting shoppers not just locally from the West Midlands but from
across all parts of the UK. If organisations are serious about increasing

engagement with diverse groups and sharing the benefits of cultural programmes with minority groups, they need to consider engaging on their terms, about topics that will attract them, through methods and venues that are convenient to them. For work with Muslim communities, this work needs to acknowledge the diversity of cultures and traditions that make up British Muslim communities. Exhibition programming should explore, and welcome, strong emotional responses to objects that have spiritual significance without dismissing or minimising the role of faith and the way it informs identity, culture and artistic output for Muslims.

One major impediment to widening access and engaging Muslim audiences in the UK with Islamic collections is the fact that the majority of Islamic collections that have dedicated spaces for display are concentrated in the galleries and museums of London. To address this, there needs to be greater provision in large cities like Birmingham where there is a large Muslim population. Birmingham has the second largest Muslim population in the UK, with more than one in five residents of Birmingham identifying as Muslim. In a city where its Muslim population has demonstrated a desire to engage with local museums and exhibitions of relevance to them, it is scandalous that there is not a permanent gallery dedicated to Islamic art. In fact, what is called for, is something much more ambitious: a dedicated museum with the space to represent the history, complexity, diversity and breadth of creativity in the literature, arts and heritage of Muslims and the Islamic world; a space that is led by the communities whose heritage it represents with programming that explores and respects the complex layers of identity of Muslims in Britain; a space that is built at a grassroots level and provides a forum for critical thinking. In Birmingham, this radical solution has been developed with the foundation of a charity – the Museum of Islamic Arts and Heritage (MIAH) Foundation – which has already gathered significant pledges of support to build the UK's first purpose-built museum dedicated to Islamic arts and heritage.[24] It aims to increase Muslim participation in the arts and cultural sector by exploring the arts, heritage and history of the Islamic world through programming that is responsive to the needs and interests of its potential audiences as it works towards its goal of building a museum that will remain relevant to the lives of future generations.

Acknowledgements

This is a revised version of a paper given at the 'MBRN Muslim Arts and Heritage' Conference at the University of Birmingham in September 2017. It has been edited to provide the further context of recent debates, further statistics to demonstrate some of the discussion points of the original paper presented at the conference and reference to developments since, such as the opening of the Faith Gallery at Birmingham Museum and Art Gallery. The author is the curator of the Mingana Collection of Middle Eastern Manuscripts at the CRL, University of Birmingham.

Notes

1 For a detailed account of one of these museums, the Museum of Islamic Art, Doha, and its efforts to reach local and international publics see: Watson, Oliver. "The Museum of Islamic Art, Doha." In *Islamic Art and the Museum: Approaches to Art and Archeology of the Muslim World in the Twenty-First Century*, edited by Benoit Junod, Georges Khalil, Stefan Weber, and Gerhard Wolf, Illustrated edition., 264–69. London: Saqi Books, 2013.

2 Victoria and Albert Museum. *Victoria and Albert Museum Annual Report and Accounts 2015–2016*. London: Victoria and Albert Museum: https://V&A-production-assets.s3.amazonaws.com/2016/10/03/10/43/32/6e5327ff-0741-44b8-b65e-53e1b4b1da0b/VAM%20Stat%20Accounts%202015-16%20FINAL(3). PDF [accessed 19 July 2022].

3 The British Museum. The British Museum: Report and Accounts for the Year Ended 31 March 2007. London: The British Museum, p.15: https://assets. publishing.service.gov.uk/government/uploads/system/uploads/attachment_data/file/250722/0777.pdf [accessed 19 July 2022]. This is the last report in which I was able to locate details of participation by ethnic minorities.

4 The full range of reports from 2006 to 2020 can be accessed at: https://www. gov.uk/government/collections/sat--2#taking-part-adult-statistical-releases [accessed 19 July 2022].

5 Peggy Levitt. 'Museums Must Attract Diverse Visitors or Risk Irrelevance'. *The Atlantic*, 9 November 2015 https://www.theatlantic.com/politics/archive/2015/11/museums-must-attract-diverse-visitors-or-risk-irrelevance/433347/ [accessed 19 July 2022].

6 Vincent Noce. 'French President Emmanuel Macron calls for International Conference on the Return of African Artefacts'. *The Art Newspaper*, 26 November 2018: https://www.theartnewspaper.com/news/french-president-emmanuel-macron-calls-for-international-conference-on-the-return-of-african-artefacts [accessed 19 July 2022].

7 Felwine Sarr and Bénédicte Savoy. *The Restitution of African Cultural Heritage: Toward a New Relational Ethics*. Ministère De La Culture, November 2018: http://restitutionreport2018.com [accessed 19 July 2022].

8 Christopher F. Schuetze. 'Germany Sets Guidelines for Repatriating Colonial-Era Artifacts'. *New York Times*, 15 March 2019: https://www.nytimes.com/2019/03/15/arts/design/germany-museums-restitution.html [accessed 19 July 2022].

9 Ahdaf Soueif. 'On Resigning from the British Museum's Board of Trustees'. *London Review of Books*, 15 July 2019: https://www.lrb.co.uk/blog/2019/july/on-resigning-from-the-british-museum-s-board-of-trustees [accessed 19 July 2022].

10 Tristram Hunt. 'Should Museums Return their Colonial Artefacts?' *The Observer*, 29 June 2019: https://www.theguardian.com/culture/2019/jun/29/should-museums-return-their-colonial-artefacts [accessed 19 July 2022].

11 Sharon Heal. 'Who's Afraid of Decolonisation?' *Museums Association*, 3 July 2019: https://www.museumsassociation.org/museums-journal/comment/03072019-whos-afraid-of-decolonisation-policy-column [accessed 19 July 2022].

12 On the decolonisation of museums see: Amy Lonetree. *Decolonizing Museums: Representing Native America in National and Tribal Museums*. Chapel Hill: University North Carolina Press, 2012. Claire Smith. 'Decolonising the

Museum: The National Museum of the American Indian in Washington, DC'. *Antiquity* 79, no. 304 (June 2005): 424–39. https://doi.org/10.1017/S0003598X00114206. For a discussion focusing on Islamic art see: Wendy M. K. Shaw. *What Is "Islamic" Art? Between Religion and Perception.* Cambridge, United Kingdom: Cambridge University Press, 2019.

13 For an overview of their work see Jasper Goss. 'Postcolonialism: Subverting Whose Empire?' *Third World Quarterly*, 17 (2), pp.239–50; Donna Landry and Gerald McLean, eds. *The Spivak Reader.* New York, NY: Routledge, 1995. See also: Homi K. Bhabha. *Location of Culture.* London: Routledge, 1994; Edward Said. *Orientalism.* New York, NY: Vintage, 1979; Edward Said. *Culture and Imperialism.* New York, NY: Vintage, 1994; Gayatri Chakravorty Spivak. *A Critique of Postcolonial Reason: Toward a History of the Vanishing Present.* New York: Routledge, 1999; Gayatri Chakravorty Spivak. *Death of a Discipline.* New York: Columbia University Press, 2005; Gayatri Chakravorty Spivak and Ranajit Guha (eds.). *Selected Subaltern Studies.* Oxford: Oxford University Press, 1988; Gayatri Chakravorty Spivak. *The Post-Colonial Critic: Interviews, Strategies, Dialogues.* New York, NY: Routledge, 1990.

14 For details see https://decolonizethisplace.org [accessed 19 July 2022].

15 For details see https://rmfoxford.wordpress.com [accessed 19 July 2022].

16 Cultural Diversity Working Group. *Cultural Diversity: Final Report and Recommendations.* National Museums Directors' Conference. March 2006: https://www.nationalmuseums.org.uk/media/documents/publications/cultural_diversity_final_report.pdf [accessed 19 July 2022]. To the best of my knowledge, the National Museum Directors Council has not produced more recent figures.

17 Kavita Bhanot. 'Decolonise, not Diversify'. *Media Diversified*, 30 December 2015: https://mediadiversified.org/2015/12/30/is-diversity-is-only-for-white-people/ [accessed 19 July 2022].

18 For details of the 'Our Shared Cultural Heritage' project see: https://oursharedculturalheritage.org [accessed 19 July 2022].

19 Sumaya Kassim. 'The Museum Will Not Be Decolonised'. *Media Diversified*, 15 November 2017: https://mediadiversified.org/2017/11/15/the-museum-will-not-be-decolonised/ [accessed 19 July 2022].

20 For details see: http://www.gwacic.com/?page_id=368 [accessed 19 July 2022].

21 Details of this exhibition can be found at: http://barber.org.uk/the-mughals-power-and-beauty-at-the-indian-court/ [accessed 19 July 2022].

22 University of Birmingham Press Office. 'Birmingham Qur'an Manuscript Dated among the Oldest in the World'. *University of Birmingham*, 22 July 2015: https://www.birmingham.ac.uk/news/latest/2015/07/quran-manuscript-22-07-15.aspx [accessed 19 July 2022].

23 Full details of the course can be found at: https://www.futurelearn.com/courses/birmingham-quran [accessed 19 July 2022].

24 See: https://www.miahfoundation.com [accessed 19 July 2022].

8 Flawed and Toxic? Challenges in Contemporary Islamic Art in the UK

Sara Choudhrey

Introduction: Stakeholders of Islamic Art

The research findings shared here involved a series of interviews with individuals who could be described as stakeholders within the field of Islamic art. The aim was to understand the perspectives of those individuals who would be considered most involved in the production and dissemination of knowledge on Islamic art or artistic production. Interviewees were engaged with making, teaching, promoting, exhibiting or collecting visual Islamic art in the UK, their occupational roles being curators, artists and scholars.

In order to ensure relevance to the subject of local influences and subsequent related themes, all interviewees were required to be actively working or residing in the UK. Further criteria for inclusion specific to artist participants required that they had previously been exhibited in the UK under the theme of 'Islamic art' or had been described as such by either themselves or their peers and curators. Artists might have even shunned this term but had a religious or spiritual link to the Islamic faith or had been identified as having heritage linked to Muslim culture or place (for example, through ethnicity, or through their own or their parents' place of birth or residence).

In all, 27 participants were interviewed – ten artists, nine curators and eight teachers and lecturers. The range of experience and knowledge amongst participants was indicated through their award-winning status, artists who had exhibited nationally and internationally, curators from museums including The British Museum, the V&A, Birmingham Museums Trust and world-class institutions such as The Courtauld Institute of Art, The Prince's Foundation School of Traditional Arts and also representatives from Arts Council England. All interview participants were given the option to remain anonymous, which some opted for and others did not. The benefit of anonymous conditions for interviews is the provision of a platform for free and open expression without liability for one's views. It was found that those who did opt for anonymity were more vocal

DOI: 10.4324/9781003330714-12

about the negative aspects they had encountered in their field. Interview content was analysed using a thematic method, where two of the key themes included the interpretation of Islamic art, and identity and representation, which will be discussed further.

Interpreting Islamic Art

With contentions in the classification of Islamic art raised by academics in the last decade,[1] the topic was incorporated into the interview questions to determine if concerns relating to terminology were specific to particular stakeholders over others. All interview participants were asked to provide a definition of Islamic art and describe what this might be. Many commented on the difficulty in defining Islamic art and provided disclaimers within their responses, providing examples that may prove to be exceptions to their descriptions.

> You can't define it, it's a bit like trying to define Marx in a way. It's still an abstract notion so you can't really nail it and say this is what it is.
>
> Anonymous interviewee A, Artist[2]

Many participants conveyed an awareness of the differing views within academia regarding terminology and definitions.[3] The use of the term 'Islamic art' carries with it a number of overlong descriptions and often includes disclaimers to explain where there may be exceptions to common academic definitions. It has also been identified as an issue that is further complicated when considering the use or allocation of this term for contemporary artistic production outside of the Islamic world.[4] Artworks associated with this classification have tended to be grouped by a particular (usually historic) time period, their origin in a region of dominant Islamic rule or the presence of a Muslim patron or audience within the locality of production. However, such academic definitions fail to account for the ever-evolving contemporary context. Examples include those where artists identify as Muslim but may produce work that is not 'Islamic' in nature, or where non-Muslim artists do produce work on subjects relating to Islamic architecture, culture or faith. The assignation of terminology based on artistic production within specific locality is further complicated by the increasing movement of people leading to diaspora communities across the globe. Artists of these communities do not have singular identities based on just their nationality or place of residence. These characteristics have been a convenient method for describing and grouping artists' work in past exhibitions, yet demonstrate an over-simplification of an individual's identity.[5]

> The definitions are flawed.
>
> Anonymous interviewee B, Artist[6]

In spite of these exceptions, it was still possible to determine cases where interview participants were comfortable to use and assign the term 'Islamic art' and cases where they deemed it inappropriate. For example, there was a greater emphasis by curators in considering the time period of an artwork's production, where only historical artefacts would be called 'Islamic art'. The 'historical' is a clear marker for the past, a period prior to the modern and contemporary, a bygone era. This correlates with the many publications on Islamic art, where the timeline of Islamic art history is discussed up to the end of the Ottoman Empire.[7] The dissolution of power and reign of perhaps what was considered a large threat to Western geopolitics at the turn of the twentieth century is implied here to have also marked the end of artistic practice associated with Islamic culture.

> I don't think you can define modern and contemporary art as Islamic.
> Anonymous interviewee C, Curator of
> Islamic and South Asian art[8]

The relevance of art history, as a field, must be accepted in shaping the views of the curators regarding the usage of terminology. 'Islamic art' is widely accepted to be a Western term introduced in the nineteenth century, used to describe artefacts originating from those regions where Islam was the dominant religion or where Muslim populations were most dominant.[9] This was a period when the Ottoman Empire still existed. It was not until the mid-twentieth century that the West had entered a transnational phase. Therefore, until the modern period, objects were still easier to associate with regional or dynastic production, originating outside of the West, in locations such as the Middle East, South and far East Asia and North Africa, i.e. the Orient.

Stakeholders' aversion to use of the term Islamic art becomes clearer in light of the external factors they are exposed to. However, it could also be related to sentiments much closer to them within the art scene. One of the curators interviewed for this study had often been described as a curator of 'modern Islamic art'. In their interview, they expressed a firm resistance to the term 'Islamic art'. Their view was that it was too religiously connected and did not do justice to the vast modern art from the Middle Eastern region. They also insisted that they 'never ask an artist what their religion is', implying a detachment or validity for religious relevance to art from the region. They went on to describe a need for religious affiliation by members of the general public to be kept a private matter. It could be understood that the aversion to the term 'Islamic art' became tied to a personal view of how society should conduct itself – without religious expression of any kind. The association of the terminology was presented by this curator as only a religious one, not one related to visual language, tradition or artistic practice in a cultural

context. In defending their stance on the narrowing effect of such terminology, this participant instead presented a limited interpretation of
the term. Although they are not alone in this view,[10] there is a general
acceptance that contemporary art and architecture can and does still
connect to Islamic tradition.[11]

Perhaps with an awareness of such sentiments, another of the interviewees, an artist, likened the word 'Islam' to having a 'toxic' effect when
used in relation to describing an artistic practice, an artwork or an exhibition. In this case, the artist was making reference to perceptions
around Islam in wider society. They feared that the potential audience of
an exhibition might be deterred from visiting due to negative mis-
conceptions they may have developed in regards to Islam and Muslims.
The choice to not use terminology here was being heavily influenced by
the actions of society specific to the locality. The artist was expressing an
awareness of behaviour, interpretation and representation relating to
external influences such as the media.

> The titles are so important in an exhibition, if you get the title wrong
> it all goes down the pan.
>
> Anonymous interviewee C

A common expression amongst participants (both artists and curators)
was that artists 'do not like labels'. This became a form of validation,
justifying why terminology such as 'Islam' and 'Islamic art' should not
be used in relation to an artist's work.

Understandably, curators face a challenge in how to present large
collections of work with some form of grouping that allows for ease of
interpretation for visitors. The goal is naturally to communicate how the
exhibited objects or artworks relate to people and society.[12] Interviewed
participants provided real-world examples of where they felt this had
either worked well or failed, specifically in the naming of museum spaces
and exhibitions. One such example of a positive, yet awkward, change to
a title was the renaming of the Islamic art galleries at The Metropolitan
Museum in New York in 2011. The new name was a lengthy 13 words:
'Art of the Arab Lands, Turkey, Iran, Central Asia, and Later South
Asia'.[13] This new title was seen as a recognition of the individual regions
of the world from which the collections were developed. Yet it is almost
tempting to find a place that might not fit with this specific list of
localities just to prove it might not be all-inclusive. In contrast, Los
Angeles Contemporary Museum of Art's choice to name their two-part
exhibition 'Islamic Art Now: Contemporary Art of the Middle East' was
not as favoured.[14] The sentiment was also widely echoed in reviews at
the time of its launch in 2015. Perhaps unsurprisingly, the problematic
aspect was the inclusion of the term 'Islamic', whereas the sub-line of

contemporary art relating to the Middle Eastern region was deemed more suitable.[15] Curator of this exhibition, Lisa Komaroff, defended her decision, explaining that the use of 'Islamic' pertained to a broader meaning, inclusive of artworks that had been shaped by Islam.

Locality and Media Representation

It comes as little surprise that the contentions surrounding terminology in academia and curation of Islamic art would filter through to those stakeholders who are 'on the ground', those producing the art. Knowledge of academic definitions, a skewed, western-centric representation of art history and the lack of more diverse representation within art spaces in the UK were some of the challenges expressed by the artists. A significant theme related to communication and the lack of wider public knowledge on Islam and Islamic art was found to run parallel to concerns regarding perceptions of Islam and Muslims as portrayed to wider society through the media.

> [T]he bad press frankly is relentless and its jolly difficult to balance it when you have quite so much coming out.
> Anonymous Interviewee D, Historian of Islamic Art[16]

To provide some further context to the interviewees and how their sentiments might be influenced, it is helpful to consider their multifaceted identities. Almost half of interview participants were of minority ethnic backgrounds but usually of first or second-generation descent. In total, 7 of 10 artists, 4 of 9 curators and 5 of 8 scholars were of non-white background; in total 16 of 27. The question of faith was not directly asked of participants; however, many divulged this either within the interviews or shared this openly through previous communications in press or with the author. At least 12 of the 27 participants were known to be Muslim. This insight provides a crucial insight into the effects of representations of Islam and Muslims in the wider public, where any repercussions are particularly felt by those artists who might engage with a public audience and be questioned about this facet of their identity.

Participants expressed a growing awareness of hostility, resentment, dislike and a negative attitude from the 'outside world' towards all things 'Islam'. It was strongly felt that the media played a large part in this and was voiced by both Muslim and non-Muslim participants.

> Everything that people believe about Islam is so awful. I can't even bring myself to read an article …, the comments below the line is just like, wow, you know, people hate us, really hate us.
> Anonymous interviewee B[17]

Studies of news media communications have shown that coverage of Muslims is in most cases presented in relation to a negative event or presenting the Muslim community in opposition to wider British society.[18] The number of articles and also their rapidity of publication (both on air and in print) has been described to have reached a momentum unprecedented for other pockets of society. This phenomenon has been compared to the concept and effects of Orientalism, where media representations of Muslims are similar to the examples of 'barbaric' representations of Arabs as discussed by Edward Said in his now famous title Orientalism in 1978.[19] The effects of such discourse and 'mis'-representation therefore propels Islamophobia and the authentic peaceful message of Islamic ideology.[20]

The increase of negative portrayals has not been lost on the Muslim community, where regardless of proudly identifying as British, Muslims increasingly feel like outsiders in the UK.[21] Examples of media articles highlighting this 'otherness' includes *The Independent*'s 'A third of Muslims say they feel under greater suspicion in the last few years'[22] and *The Telegraph*'s 'One in Three Muslims do not Feel Part of British Culture'.[23] In the wake of Brexit, a majority public vote for Britain to leave the EU encouraged by campaigns focused on problems in Britain due to mass immigration and multiculturalism, the focus on Muslims in relation to societal concerns on 'Britishness' has not dissipated.[24]

The Role of the Artist

In such situations, the media has sought responses from those within the Muslim community to express their 'side'. Although the participating artists in this research mentioned that they were often placed on pedestals by members of the Muslim community to which they are (sometimes loosely) affiliated, they also felt they had to live up to certain expectations of appearing like or behaving like other Muslims. The concept of representation was therefore one that touched on the private and personal lives of the artists as well as their public-facing identities.

However, being appointed as a representative provides an opportunity to carry a voice further afield. This was demonstrated through an article published by *The Guardian*, 'Art gets things out in the Open – Young British Muslim artists tell their stories',[25] where four artists of Muslim heritage were invited to speak on the topic of 'Cultural tensions in the UK over the past 15 years'. These artists were asked to what degree they felt responsible to use their voices to counter negative stereotypes faced by young British Muslims. The opportunity to be interviewed for a national paper provided these artists with a platform and amplified their voice for responding to the negative rhetoric and widespread misunderstanding amongst the general public regarding the

Muslim community. It also gave insight into the personal impact these sentiments and expressions had on the artists when national and international attacks were carried out in the name of Islam and Muslims. The street artist Mohammed Ali described the incorporation of surveillance cameras in his work after the government proposed to increase CCTV in response to the Charlie Hebdo attacks in Paris in 2015. Also, interviewed for the article, playwright and actor Yusra Warsama mentioned the impact of the 11 September attacks, the Iraq war and changes experienced by Muslims in Britain between then and now.

Artists of minority backgrounds have been tackling topics of marginalisation and negative public sentiment towards their communities for decades in the UK.[26] Rasheed Araeen, a Pakistani artist who settled in the UK in the 1970s, was a member of the British Black Panther movement. In 1990, he installed Golden Verses, a large billboard poster printed with an image of a rug containing writing in Urdu script.[27] The style of the script was calligraphic, reminiscent of the Arabic Qur'anic script. Therefore, the appearance of the work alone would meet the criteria of Islamic art based on the visual language alone.

The text in the artwork read:

WHITE PEOPLE ARE VERY GOOD PEOPLE. THEY HAVE VERY WHITE AND SOFT SKIN. THEIR HAIR IS GOLDEN AND THEIR EYES ARE BLUE. THEIR CIVILISATION IS THE BEST CIVILISATION. IN THEIR COUNTRIES THEY LIVE LIFE WITH LOVE AND AFFECTION. AND THERE IS NO RACIAL DISCRIMINATION WHATSOEVER. WHITE PEOPLE ARE VERY GOOD PEOPLE.[28]

By incorporating a stereotypical description of the appearance of white western people from the perspective of a non-Western viewer, yet in a language that can only be read by a minority group of society, the artwork became an instant provocation. At the time, most non-Urdu reading viewers who were familiar with the visual style of Arabic script assumed the text was a sample of verses from the Qur'an. The work caused some controversy due to members of the Muslim community assuming that the verses were being used in a disrespectful manner. From the far right, non-Muslims expressed their discontent through graffiti over the work, spouting their concerns that British culture was being invaded. This rhetoric is not dissimilar to that found in the media today.[29] Art can therefore be used to provoke and encourage discussions, but public sentiments and retaliation cannot always be predicted.

Artists have not been discouraged by the negative rhetoric, instead using art as a means to encourage a more positive perception and means to open dialogue. Artist Saba Rifat, who also leads Islamic geometric workshops, ran a series in Dewsbury with the intention of engaging the locals in friendly and open dialogue.[30] The format of these workshops involved colouring geometric patterns and bringing people from varied backgrounds together through a simple and enjoyable creative activity. Rifat was able to use this opportunity to draw in new audiences and to broach the subject of integration in response to recent tensions between what was felt by locals to be differing in pockets of society.[31]

Although shedding a positive light on the use of art as a method for community cohesion, there is an implication that it is the responsibility of artists closely related to the Muslim community to raise awareness and dispel ignorance for the wider public. They become not just models for the community they are most associated with but they must be the saviours too. Yet, despite being British-born, residents and nationals of the UK, artists engaging with Islamic art or Islamic visual culture are not deemed as fitting into wider British identity.

Art is an emotive and expressive endeavour and therefore the experiences of an artist cannot be detached from their work or the role they play within society. However, being a minority part of that society may lead to specific decisions made by artists in response to how they are perceived by their audience. Mohammed Ali is still asked to discuss art, Muslims and integration. In a recent post on social media, he shared news of a documentary being filmed by Al-Jazeera. He states he has 'Done this topic to death with media for nearly two decades' but remains hopeful of new insights.[32]

Conclusion

The anonymised interviewing of stakeholders of Islamic art in the UK provided a unique opportunity to open discussions on topics relating to challenges within the local Islamic art scene. Stakeholders of Islamic art were shown to be tied to both the social and political climate of their locality where, in the case of anything related to Islam and Muslims, the rhetoric is at the mercy of the media.

Artists, however, faced a larger number of challenges, shown to be particularly pressured into a role where they must answer to and for their associated Muslim community and also provide a solution to address fears regarding that community. Added to this pressure, the artist must also navigate public sentiment in the context of situating themselves within both the local and wider art scene. Choices are made regarding the use of terminology in describing art and artistic practice that might be considered invalid to their peers and patrons. Their choices cannot be isolated from the opinions held by curators and academics, to whom they are at the additional mercy of.

Curators and academics of the Islamic art scene perhaps need to be more accepting of both broad and specific interpretations of the long-standing term 'Islamic art'. As long as artists continue to produce what they have the right to term as Islamic art, the continued usage of the term in the contemporary context must also be accepted, regardless of religious affiliation being openly or discreetly presented.

By allowing for the term 'contemporary' to refer to art relating to Islam is acknowledging contemporary artistic expression which has a long and rich heritage. It is presenting an opportunity for the continuity in Islamic art to be accepted by existing and new audiences, validating that it is current and relevant. This might be especially effective in a locality where Islam might be presented with a voice from outside of the Muslim community and to its detriment.

Notes

1 Sheila S. Blair and Jonathan M. Bloom. 'The Mirage of Islamic Art: Reflections on the Study of an Unwieldy Field'. *The Art Bulletin*, 83 (1), 2004, pp. 152–184.

2 Interviewed by author, November 2015.

3 On the conceptual parameters of the category of Islamic art in academic scholarship see: Wendy Shaw. 'The Islam in Islamic Art History: Secularism and Public Discourse'. *Journal of Art Historiography*, 6, 2012, pp. 1–34.

4 Sarah Choudhrey. *Pigment to Pixel: An Investigation into Digital Islamic Art in the UK.* Doctor of Philosophy (PhD) thesis, University of Kent, 2018.

5 Fereshteh Daftari. 'Islamic or Not'. In *Without Boundary: Seventeen Ways of Looking*, 10–27. New York: Museum of Modern Art, 2006.

6 Interviewed by author, September 2015.

7 Finbarr Barry Flood. 'From Prophet to Postmodernism? New World Orders and the End of Islamic Art'. In Elizabeth Mansfield (ed.), *Making Art History: A Changing Discipline and its Institutions*. London: Routledge, 2007, pp. 31-53. On the neglect of modern and contemporary art from the Arab world in art history, see Nada M. Shabout. *Modern Arab Art: Formation of Arab Aesthetics.* Gainesville: University Press of Florida, 2015.

8 Interviewed by author September 2015.

9 Chela Weitzel. 'The Written Word in Islamic Art'. In *The Buddha of Suburbia: Proceedings of the Eighth Australian and International Religion, Literature and the Arts Conference*, 213-222. Sydney, Australia: RLA Press, 2004: https://openjournals.library.sydney.edu.au/index.php/SSR/article/view/114/134 [accessed 12 February 2019].

10 Nada M. Shabout. 'What's in a Name? Contemplating the "Islamic" in the "contemporary"'. In Tim Stanly and Salma Tuqan (eds.) *Jameel Prize 4.* Istanbul: Pera Muzesi Yayini, 2016, pp.12-19.

11 F. Jameel. (2016). 'Foreword'. In Tim Stanly and Salma Tuqan (eds.) *Jameel Prize 4.* Istanbul: Pera Muzesi Yayini, 2016, p. 11.

12 Sheila Bergman. Perspectives, Approaches, and Experiences in Curating Contemporary Art: A Phenomenographic Study. Doctoral Dissertation, Fielding Graduate University, 2015.

13 The Metropolitan Museum of Art. 'Metropolitan Museum to Open Renovated Galleries for the Art of the Arab Lands, Turkey, Iran, Central Asia, and Later

South Asia'. *The Met*, 2011: *Accessed* 12 February 2019, https://www. metmuseum.org/press/exhibitions/2011/renovated-galleries-for-the-art-of-the-arab-lands-turkey-iran-central-asia-and-later-south-asia [accessed 12 February 2019].

14 Rose Issa. 'Figures of Protest in Contemporary Arab and Iranian Art'. In Christiane Gruber (ed.) *The Image Debate*. London: Gingko Library, pp. 212–227.

15 Susan Stamberg. 'At LA Museum, A Powerful and Provocative Look at "Islamic Art Now"'. *NPR*, 5 May 2015: https://www.npr.org/2015/05/05/402642797/at-la-museum-a-powerful-and-provocative-look-at-islamic-art-now [accessed 20 July 2022].

16 Interviewed by author January 2016.

17 Interviewed by author September 2015.

18 Justin Lewis, Paul Mason and Kerry Moore. 'Images of Islam in the UK: The Representation of British Muslims in the National Print News Media 2000-2008'. In Julian Petley and Robin Richardson (eds.) *Pointing the Finger: Islam and Muslims in the British Media*. Oxford: Oneworld Publications, 2011, pp. 40–65.

19 Elizabeth Poole. *Reporting Islam: Media Representations of British Muslims*. London: I.B Tauris, 2002.

20 Shah Nister Kabir, Sharifah Nurul Huda Alkaff and Michael Bourk. 'Iconizing "Muslim Terrorism" in a British Newspaper and Public Perception'. *Journal of Muslim Minority Affairs*, 38 (2), 2018, pp.179-197; Noureddine Miladi. 'The Discursive Representation of Islam and Muslims in the British Tabloid Press'. *Journal of Applied Journalism & Media Studies*, 10 (1), 2021, pp. 117–138.

21 Mohammed Ali. @aliaerosol via Instagram, 2019: https://www.instagram.com/aliaerosol/ [accessed 20 July 2022].

22 Kashmira Gander. 'A Third of Muslims Say They Feel under Greater Suspicion in the Last Few Years, Survey Shows'. *The Independent*, 10 April 2015: https://www.independent.co.uk/news/uk/home-news/a-third-of-muslims-say-they-feel-under-greater-suspicion-in-the-last-few-years-survey-shows-10168449.html [accessed 20 July 2022].

23 John Bingham. 'One in Three Muslims Do Not Feel "Part of British Culture"'. *The Telegraph*, 23 May 2016: https://www.telegraph.co.uk/news/2016/05/26/one-in-three-muslims-do-not-feel-part-of-british-culture/ [accessed 20 July 2022].

24 Richard Ashcroft and Mark Bevir. 'Pluralism, National Identity and Citizenship: Britain after Brexit'. *Political Quarterly*, 87 (3), 2016, pp. 355-359; Laleh Khalili. 'After Brexit: Reckoning with Britain's Racism and Xenophobia'. *Poem*, 5 (2–3), 2017, pp. 253–265.

25 Tim Adams. '"Art Gets Things Out in the Open" – Young British Muslim Artists Tell their Stories'. *The Guardian*, 12 April 2015: https://www.theguardian.com/culture/2015/apr/12/young-british-muslim-artists-mohammed-ali-aveas-mohammad-yusra-warsama-aisha-zia [accessed 20 July 2022].

26 Rasheed Araeen. 'The Success and the Failure of Black Art'. *Third Text*, 18 (2), 2004, pp. 135–152.

27 Rasheed Araeen. 'The Artist as a Post-Colonial Subject and this Individual's Journey Towards "the Centre"'. In Catherine King (ed.) *Views of Difference: Different Views of Art*. New Haven: Yale University Press, 1999, pp. 229–255.

28 Ibid.

29 The Independent. 'Third of Brexit Voters Believe Muslim Immigration is Part of a Secret Plot to Islamicise Britain, Study Suggests'. *Independent*, 23 November 2018: https://www.independent.co.uk/news/uk/home-news/brexit-voters-immigration-muslims-islam-leave-remain-yougov-survey-trump-a8648586.html [accessed 20 July 2022].

30 Saba Rifat. 'Geometric Friends', Art Installation Launch Event. 21 April 2019: http://www.sabarifat.co.uk/geometric-friends-art-installation-launch-may-14th-2016/ [accessed 20 July 2022].

31 Eve Hartley and George Bowden. 'This Muslim Artist is Bringing Divided Communities Together using Seriously Cool Art'. *Huffington Post*, 16 February 2017: http://www.huffingtonpost.co.uk/entry/dewsbury-muslim-artist-geometric-friends_uk_58a570d9e4b037d17d24e8d1 [accessed 20 July 2022].

32 Sundas Ali. *British Muslims in Numbers: A Demographic, Socio-Economic and Health Profile of Muslims in Britain Drawing on the 2011 Census*. London: Muslim Council of Britain, 2015.

Conclusion

The Future of British Muslim Arts

Sadek Hamid and Stephen H. Jones

The contributions to this volume amply show that British Muslim art is a field marked by a multiplicity of cross-cutting tensions. It is transnational, drawing on traditions from across the world, yet also localised, taking the form of distinctively British or even London-based styles, like Grime. Its location on the cultural and institutional margins enables it to offer powerful critiques of British society, yet it seeks – and sometimes finds – recognition in venerated and influential cultural institutions. It can be highly conservative, offering a 'halal' alternative to Western popular culture, but also hosts British Islam's most progressive voices, giving space to those who are marginal to Muslim institutions on account of their gender, sexuality or religious views. Much British Muslim art continues traditions that are thousands of years old, yet these can be – as in the case of Razwan ul-Haq – fused with contemporary visual styles or manipulated by digital technology. Perhaps most importantly, it can be presented in the secularised form in mainstream exhibitions, but, as in the case of most of the artists contributing to this collection, it is often understood by artists themselves as a devotional activity. These tensions often intersect, with British Muslim art's religiosity being – as we saw in the case of Sara Choudhrey's contribution to this collection– one of the main reasons why it remains on the margins of cultural institutions.

Such tensions go some way towards explaining why it is hard to pin down British Muslim art by setting out its essential characteristics. Beyond being created by people who self-identify as Muslims and who reside in the UK, there often seems to be little that unites it. This volume has sought to show, however, that British Muslim arts can be described not just in terms of distinguishing characteristics but also in terms of *cultural change*. British Muslim art can be seen, that is, as one chapter in an important story about the embedding of Muslims and Islam in Britain. Despite facing social deprivation, securitisation and housing and health inequalities, British Muslims make increasing contributions to the UK's economic, educational and cultural fabric, with this growing due

DOI: 10.4324/9781003330714-13

to younger generations entering higher professions in greater numbers.[1] Contrary to moral panics about 'self-segregation', Muslims – and Muslim institutions – are becoming ever more part of the country's mainstream. Over 10% of NHS doctors are Muslim and around 40,000 Muslims work in various capacities in the NHS.[2] During the COVID-19 crisis, British Muslims were on the frontline in healthcare, as well as providing food banks, reaching out to the vulnerable and using mosques as mortuaries.[3] This is supported by a thriving British Muslim charitable sector, which is maintained by an estimated £500 million per annum in donations.[4] Within the sphere of civil society, a constellation of British Muslim activists and lobbying groups engage with the state in increasingly sophisticated ways.[5] Even in the Islamic education sector, which emerged in the UK in the 1970s and 1980s to maintain South Asian and Middle Eastern Islamic traditions for future generations, one can find striking changes, with many institutions reorienting themselves and developing more and deeper ties with universities and further education colleges across Britain.[6]

Using the chapters in this volume, it is possible to see how British Muslim art forms part of this process of Islam and Muslims becoming a more fundamental part of the social and civil structures of British liberal democracy. The sector has followed common patterns, with increasing engagement described being driven by generational change. The landscape of British Islamic education has altered largely because of a maturing generation of UK-born Islamic scholars reorienting their educational institutions in order to meet students' demands for relevant and useful qualifications. In much the same way, a rising generation of British Muslims is using art to directly challenge Muslim institutions and UK society. This generation has often utilised vocabularies of anti-racism, decolonisation and Islamic activism, as Shaheen Kasmani's chapter illustrates. There is, however, much more to this challenge that the somewhat tired stereotype of disaffected young British Muslims equally alienated by mosque and British public culture. Generational change among the Muslim arts scene is now sufficiently advanced that Muslim traditions are being refashioned into new institutional and aesthetic forms (such as 'post-*tariqa* Sufism', described in Ayesha Khan's chapter), while an established cohort of Muslim professionals can find limited space and influence in established arts institutions (as we can see in Neelam Hussain's chapter, or in examples such as the Arts Council's 'Arts and Islam' initiative).[7]

This is not to say, of course, that the situation for British Muslim art and artists is positive or the pathway forward looks smooth. We noted at the beginning of this volume that media portrayals of British Muslims are overwhelmingly negative,[8] with the national media outlets frequently reinforcing anti-Muslim tropes and distorting stories.[9] This general climate of negativity impacts Muslims in every sphere of British society, limiting employment outcomes and life chances.[10] It affects the arts too, but here there are additional difficulties. Unlike many spheres of British society, such as political activism or charity, where a Muslim presence is relatively recent, Muslim art has long had a presence in the British cultural sector and features today in major exhibitions. Some of the finest artefacts in the Victoria and Albert Museum, for example, are of Muslim cultural heritage, with over 19,000 items coming from the Middle East and North Africa. This is one of 17 museums across Europe and the Mediterranean that participated in the 'Discover Islamic Art' project developed by the Brussels-based consortium 'Museum With No Frontiers' and showcased over 1,200 works of Islamic art in an online virtual museum.[11] As scholars such as Wendy Shaw and Jessica Winegar, have observed however – as well as Kasmani and Choudhrey in their chapters – this inclusion can reinforce rather than combat prejudices. Britain's encounter with Islamic art took place against a backdrop of colonial interventions in Muslim-majority states, and this history continues to influence the sector, with Islamic art presented in a secularised vocabulary that exoticizes Muslim traditions. Many artistic exhibits of the 'Islamic world' were stimulated directly by the events of 11 September 2001,[12] and even when they were set up to bridge cultural divides frequently they have done the opposite by, in Shaw's words, 'reflecting the glories of "Islamic" culture as part of a bygone golden age, or by suggesting that the appropriate environment for religion (and in particular Islam) rests in the past rather than in the present'.[13] It is unsurprising, then, that a common theme of not only Kasmani and Choudhrey's contributions but also the chapters by Mahamdallie and Neelam Hussain is that meaningfully including British Muslims' art in the mainstream typically means engaging with, and pushing back against, traditions that refuse Muslims the space to engage in the sector as interlocutors rather than subjects of enquiry.

Given this, it should be no surprise that British Muslim art has often aligned itself with radical and decolonial politics, or that it finds a home in urban counter-culture as well as elite cultural institutions. The Black Lives Matter (BLM) movement has added momentum to long-standing calls to openly discuss the brutal hidden histories behind many British cultural institutions and iconic figures.[14] These protests and growing social momentum may succeed in pressuring British museums to return looted items by following the example of the Ethnological Museum of Berlin, which recently transferred hundreds of the Benin Bronzes to Nigeria.[15] Such radical and decolonial movements, however, easily find themselves drawn into a fierce culture war focused on the removal of statues or teaching British imperial history – especially when they start to influence established national institutions. One vivid example of this from the UK's cultural sector is the outrage engendered by a National Trust report on colonialism and historic slavery, which was attacked by Conservative MPs and sections of the press for documenting the UK's colonial connections to 93 historic places and collections linked to the global slave trade and the East India Company.[16] While it is encouraging to see Muslim artists given opportunities to exhibit in mainstream Museums and access community grant awarding initiatives – such as Amal and the Aziz Foundation, highlighted in Hussain's chapter – British Muslim art remains the site of potentially explosive cultural tensions. Furthermore, as Mahamdallie's chapter vividly illustrates, the widespread securitisation of Muslim communities means Muslim artistic production is all too easily caught up in destructive controversies over terrorism and the limits of free speech, leaving Muslims in a precarious position throughout the UK arts sector.

Despite these profound challenges, British Muslim artists and their interlocutors can, and do, draw on other historical sources for inspiration, notably the deep legacies which precede the predatory colonial relationships between Britain and the Muslim world. Historically, Jews, Christians and Muslims lived together during long periods of peaceful co-existence in Europe, not only in Muslim Spain but also under the Ottoman Empire and in post-Ottoman contexts such as Bosnia, Albania, Bulgaria and Crimea. Islamic civilisation has enriched the continent in various domains including language, maths, science, philosophy, architecture, and literature and has shaped Western civilisation in foundational ways.[17] In language, words such as admiral, algebra, alchemy and alcohol are all derived from Arabic words imported into Europe during the Crusades.[18] Many Western musical instruments, such as the lute, guitar and violin, were copied from instruments used by touring singers, musicians and poets who visited Christian towns and villages in northern Spain, southern France and Italy.[19] In her ground-breaking study *Stealing from the Saracens: How Islamic Architecture Shaped Europe*, Diana Drake reveals the Arab and Islamic roots of Europe's architectural heritage and points out that ideas and styles from Damascus, Baghdad and Cairo travelled to Europe via Muslim Spain, Venice and Sicily and even inspired Christopher Wren's 'Saracen' style of Gothic architecture. Without the massive contributions of Muslim philosophers, physicians, scientists, artists and translators, there would have been no Renaissance – the sources of the Enlightenment are not simply in Greece and Rome, but can also be traced to Muslim civilisations.[20]

Also noteworthy are the forgotten histories of trade, diplomatic and migratory exchanges between Britain and the Muslim world from the seventh century which Martin Pugh demonstrated in his recent book *Britain and Islam: The History from 622 to the Present Day*.[21] Historians such as Nabil Matar have written extensively on various periods of interaction between different Muslim empires and England.[22] Jerry Brotton, in his book *This Orient Isle: Elizabethan England and the Islamic World*, traces the links during the Elizabethan period and shows that awareness of the Muslim cultures influenced many great English cultural productions of the day – most notably Shakespeare's *Othello* and *The Merchant of Venice* – illustrating that England's relations with the Muslim world were far more extensive and amicable, than is generally acknowledged.[23] Furthermore, fascinating new research uncovered by the archaeologist Caitlin Green has identified accounts of trade in the thirteenth and fourteenth centuries that suggest that tin from Cornwall and Devon was exported via southern France to both Egypt and ultimately Iran to be used by potters to make tin-opacified ceramic glazes.[24] These facts confirm the adaptive potential of Islam to different social contexts and possibilities for mutual cultural enrichment.

Considering this broader historical context is important when thinking about the challenges and opportunities for Muslim arts and culture in Britain in the next decade and beyond. The future of the British Muslim artistic sector will be tied to the internal conditions of the Muslim community and its relationships with the external dynamics of wider society. One can predict confidently that both the arts and Muslim Britain will remain in flux. According to the curator Jeffreen M Hayes, 'art in the future will likely become more representative of our global growing and shifting demographics, so more artists will be of colour, more female-identified works, and everything in between'.[25] Mediums of artistic expression will continue to morph into new forms that integrate new technologies such as 3D printing, virtual reality and augmented reality that offer viewers immersive artwork experiences.[26] Global interconnectivity will continue to shape the tastes and types of Islamicate art and cultural trends that are consumed by new Muslim youth cultures – particularly as 'Generation Alpha' become teenagers and Generation Z and Millennials age and influence youthscapes in different ways. Hybridisation and cross-fertilisation will increase in our networked world, generating new iterations of Muslim creativity. We are also likely to see the growth of new institutions dedicated to Islamic art such as the Aga Khan Museum in Toronto, the Islamic Arts Museum, Malaysia and the Museum of Islamic Arts and Heritage Foundation, which aims to establish Britain's first dedicated museum of Islamic art.[27] The Muslim population of the UK is set to grow at about twice the rate of the non-Muslim population, with some areas of London, as well as Leicester and Bradford, potentially having slight Muslim majorities by 2030.[28] Not only in the UK but across Western Europe people tend to drastically overestimate the size of their country's Muslim population, which is an unfortunate testament to the effectiveness of fearmongering about Muslim 'demographic replacement'.[29] Even if prophesies about 'Eurabia' can be discounted, however, it is inevitable that Islam will become more prominent among the moral traditions that make up British liberal democracy, and that Muslims' presence across various social domains – including the arts – will deepen.

In future, with this steady population growth, we are likely to see further shifts in the internal dynamics concerning the place of arts and culture within Muslim communities, resulting in new religious norms that may either see an increasing accommodationist consensus developing among scholarly communities who realise the value of arts, or potentially prohibitionist tendencies among more conservative voices. These internal barriers will need to be negotiated in order for more positive aspects of Muslim artistic endeavour to garner acceptance and greater financial support from the mainstream arts industry. While many of the authors in this volume highlighted challenges and identified the discriminatory ways in which they are excluded from the mainstream arts sector, progress is being made and we are hopeful that British Muslim art might leave lasting legacies that echo and draw upon histories of inter-religious and inter-cultural exchange. Hopeful indications of this are found in the more imaginative examples of mosque architecture such as the Cambridge Mosque, which in 2019 became the UK's 'first green mosque', and intends to act as cultural bridge for Islam in Britain in the twenty-first century. Many other creative examples have been highlighted in Shahed Saleem's colourful survey *The British Mosque: An Architectural and Social History*, which illustrates the earliest forms in the late nineteenth century and the modern mosques being built today.[30] A shared universal appreciation for such artistic beauty is one route to increasing mutual understanding, and reducing fear and conflict.

This should not be read, however, merely as a call for the 'domestication' of Islam into a simple, celebratory story of harmonious coexistence and national contribution. What makes British Muslim art remarkable and worthy of attention is that it challenges settled public norms and societal prejudices, even as it makes a claim upon space in mainstream industries and institutions. It asks penetrating questions about British society, unsettling – potentially in productive ways – established historical narratives and settlements concerning place of religiosity in British public life. As the 'playground for dangerous ideas', it carries the potential not only to reshape Muslim communal identity and norms but the national identity and institutions in the UK and beyond. If Islam and Muslim culture are to be successfully recognised as a significant part of Britain's cultural riches, then this will be by grappling productively with the tensions that run through British Muslim art – which, in the end, reflect tensions that haunt Western democracies generally.

Notes

1   See Chapter 2 in Stephen H Jones. *Islam and the Liberal State: National Identity and the Future of Muslim Britain.* London: Bloomsbury/IB Tauris, 2021.

2   NHS Statistics, 'NHS Workforce Statistics: September 2019'. *NHS Digital*: https://digital.nhs.uk/data-and-information/publications/statistical/nhs-workforce-statistics/september-2019 [accessed 15 July 2022].

3   The All-Party Parliamentary Group on British Muslims. *Rising to the Challenge: A Community's Response to Covid-19.* London: APPG on British Muslims, 2021: https://static1.squarespace.com/static/599c3d2febbd1a90cffdd8a9/t/6024f9393494 f933784903f7/1613035848097/APPG+Rising+to+the+challenge+final+(1).pdf [accessed 15 July 2022].

4   Howard Lake. 'An Introduction to Muslim Giving in the UK'. *UK Fundraising*, 6 January 2020: https://fundraising.co.uk/2020/01/06/an-introduction-to-muslim-giving-in-the-uk/#:~:text=The%20Muslim%20community's%20value%20to,the %20world%2C%20including%20the%20UK [accessed 20 July 2022].

5   Stephen H Jones. *Islam and the Liberal State: National Identity and the Future of Muslim Britain.* London: Bloomsbury/IB Tauris, 2021.

6   Sophie Gilliat-Ray. 'From "Closed Worlds" to "Open Doors": (Now) Accessing Deobandi Darul Uloom in Britain'. *Fieldwork in Religion* 13 (2), 2018, pp. 127–50.

7   'Arts and Islam' was a project set up in the early 2010s that sought to 'examine the connections between Islam, arts practice and contemporary society'. Arts Council England. Annual review 2010: Arts Council England Grant-in-aid and Lottery Annual Report and Accounts 2009/10. London: Arts Council England, 2011, p. 62: https://www.artscouncil.org.uk/sites/default/files/download-file/Arts%20Council%20England%20Annual %20review%202010.pdf [accessed 28 July 2022].

8   These tend to be a cluster of complex social problems which include grooming gangs, violent extremism, forced marriages and honour killings. For an analysis, see Claire Alexander. 'The Muslim Question(s): Reflections from a Race and Ethnic Studies Perspective'. In Claire Alexander, Victoria Redclift and Ajmal Hussain (eds.) *The New Muslims.* London: Runnymede Trust, p. 6.

9   Michael B. Munnik. 'Reaching Out in a Climate of Negativity: Perceptions and Persistence among Muslim Sources Engaging with News Media'. *Contemporary Islam* 12 (3), 2018, pp. 211–227; Centre for Media Monitoring. *British Media's Coverage of Muslims & Islam (2018–2020).* London: Centre for Media Monitoring, 2021.

10 Nabil Khattab and Tariq Modood. 'Both Ethnic and Religious: Explaining Employment Penalties Across 14 Ethno-Religious Groups in the United Kingdom'. *Journal for the Scientific Study of Religion* 54 (3), 2015, pp. 501–522.

11 See https://islamicart.museumwnf.org/. The British Museum also hosted an exhibition entitled 'Inspired by the East: How the Islamic World Influenced Western Art' on display between October 2019 and 26 January 2020: https://www.britishmuseum.org/exhibitions/inspired-east-how-islamic-world-influenced-western-art.

12 Jessica Winegar. "The Humanity Game: Art, Islam, and the War on Terror." *Anthropological Quarterly* 81 (3), 2008, pp. 651–81. https://doi.org/10.1353/anq.0.0024.

13 Shaw, Wendy. "The Islam in Islamic Art History: Secularism and Public Discourse." *Journal of Art Historiography* 6 (June 1), 2012, p. 2.

14 For substantial treatments of this subject area see Dan Hicks. *The Brutish Museums: The Benin Bronzes, Colonial Violence and Cultural Restitution*. London: Pluto Press, 2020; Alice Procter. *The Whole Picture*. London: Cassell, 2020, Fatima Manji, *Hidden Heritage: Rediscovering Britain's Lost Love of The Orient*. Chatto & Windus, 2021. These texts provide a critical examination of the accepted narratives about art on display in British museums, galleries, and stately homes.

15 Philip Oltermann, 'Berlin's Plan to Return Benin Bronzes Piles Pressure on UK Museums'. *The Guardian*, 23 March 2021: https://www.theguardian.com/artanddesign/2021/mar/23/berlins-plan-to-return-benin-bronzes-piles-pressure-on-uk-museums [accessed 15 July 2022].

16 See Sally-Anne Huxtable, Corinne Fowler, Christo Kefalas, and Emma Slocombe (eds.). *Interim Report on the Connections between Colonialism and Properties now in the Care of the National Trust, Including Links with Historic Slavery*. London: National Trust, 2020. For coverage of how the celebratory view of British history and heritage sector was recruited into a war against 'woke culture', see Jessica Murry. 'Politicians Should Not "Weaponise" UK History, says Colonialism Researcher'. *The Guardian*, 22 February 2020: https://www.theguardian.com/culture/2021/feb/22/politicians-should-not-weaponise-uk-history-says-colonialism-researcher [accessed 15 July 2022].

17 See for example, Franco Cardini. *Europe and Islam*. Oxford: Blackwell Publishing, 2001; Montgomery, W, Watt. *The Influence of Islam on Medieval Europe*. Edinburgh: Edinburgh University Press, 2004.

18 John M. Hobson. *The Eastern Origins of Western Civilisation*. Cambridge: Cambridge University Press, 2004.

19 Rabah Saoud. *The Arab Contribution to Music of the Western World*. FSTC Limited, 2004: https://muslimworldmusicday.com/files/music.pdf [accessed 15 July 2022]. An in-depth exploration can be found in Henry George Farmer. *Historical Facts for the Arabian Musical Influence*. Ayer Publishing, 1988.

20 For more see Samar Attar. *The Vital Roots of European Enlightenment: Ibn Tufayl's Influence on Modern Western thought*. Lanham: Lexington Books, 2007.

21 Martin Pugh. *Britain and Islam: The History from 622 to the Present Day*. New Haven: Yale University Press, 2019.

22 For example, see Nabil Matar. *Islam in Britain, 1558–1685*. Cambridge: Cambridge University Press, 2008; Gerald McLean. *Britain and the Islamic World, 1558–1713*. Oxford: Oxford University Press, 2011.

23 Jerry Brotton. *This Orient Isle: Elizabethan England and the Islamic World*. Penguin, 2017.

24 Caitlin Green. 'Some Arabic and Persian Accounts of the Export of Tin from Cornwall to Egypt and Iran in the Thirteenth and Fourteenth Centuries'. 27 November 2020: https://www.caitlingreen.org/2020/11/arabic-and-persian-accounts-of-cornish-tin-trade.html [accessed 15 July 2022].

25 Hayes quoted in Devon Van Houten Maldonado. 'What Will Art Look Like in 20 Years?' *BBC Culture*, 23 April 2019: https://www.bbc.com/culture/article/20190418-what-will-art-look-like-in-20-years [accessed 15 July 2022].

26 See the varies predictions in Nick Hastreiter. 'What's The Future of Art?' Future of Everything, no date: https://www.futureofeverything.io/future-art/#:~:text=%E2%80%9CArt%20clearly%20has%0a%20future,utilising%20a%20headset%20or%20phone [accessed 15 July 2022].

27 N.A. Mansour. 'Is there an Islamic Arts Revival?' *The New Arab*, 28 April 2022: https://english.alaraby.co.uk/features/there-islamic-arts-revival [accessed 20 July 2022].

28 Brian J. Grim and Mehtab S. Karim. *The Future Global Muslim Population: Projections for 2010–2030*. Washington DC: Pew Research Center Forum on Religion & Public Life, 2011, p.13: file:///C:/Users/jonessh/Downloads/FutureGlobalMuslimPopulation-WebPDF-Feb10.pdf [accessed 15 July 2022]. See also Emily McFarlan Miller. 'Europe's Muslim Population Growing – But Won't be a Majority Anytime Soon'. *Religion News Service*, 29 November 2017: http://religionnews.com/2017/11/29/europes-muslim-population-growing-but-wont-be-a-majority-anytime-soon/ [accessed 15 July 2022].

29 Pamela Duncan. 'Europeans Greatly Overestimate Muslim Population, Poll Shows'. *The Guardian*, 13 December 2016: https://www.theguardian.com/society/datablog/2016/dec/13/europeans-massively-overestimate-muslim-population-poll-shows [accessed 15 July 2022].

30 Shahed Saleem. *The British Mosque: An Architectural and Social History*. Swindon: Historic England, 2018.

Index

Abdulrashid, Nabil 9
Adam, Saif 24
African American arts 23–25, 27, 88
Aga Khan Museum, Toronto 93, 124
Ahmed, Riz 8, 30, 73
Akhtar, Ayad 89
al-Ghazali, Muhammad 6
Al Yaqoubi, Muhammad 62
Ali ibn Abi Talib 34
Ali, Mohammed (artist) 24, 115–116
Ali, Muhammad (boxer) 2
All-Party Parliamentary Group for
    Religious Literacy in the
    Media 71
Anti-Black prejudice 9
Araeen, Rasheed 115
architecture 4, 123
Aristotelian logic 51
Arts Council England 15, 85, 109
Attia, Kader 5
Aziz Foundation 123
Azmat, Sadia 24

Babikir, Ahmed 62
Bakhtiar, Laleh 38
Baldwin, Stanley 88
Barber Institute of Fine Arts 101
Baraka, Amiri 23, 25
Barelvi Muslims 13, 59, 64
Barron, Lee 69, 72
Bayt al-Fann 7
Begum, Shamima 85
Belal, Muslim (rapper) 5
Benaki Museum, Athens 93
Benin Bronzes 95–96, 122
Bey, Yasiin See Def, Mos
Bhaba, Homi 97
Bible 72

Bin Laden, Osama 83–84
Birmingham Museum and Art
    Gallery 98
Birmingham Museums Trust 109
Birmingham Qur'an See Mingana
    Collection of Middle Eastern
    Manuscripts
Black Arts Movement (BAM) 23–26,
    28–29
Black Lives Matter 29, 122
Black Muslims 9
Black Nationalism 26
Black Panther movement 115
Black Pentecostalism 71
Boal, Augusto 87
British Museum 93–94, 96, 109
British Muslim Arts Movement
    31–32, 120
British Muslim community 6; and class
    86–87; exlusion of 7; and
    generational change 6, 7, 60,
    65, 121; population growth
    124; settlement patterns 58–59
Brotton, Jerry 124
Bulliet, Richard 4
Burckhardt, Titus 4, 38, 53

Cadbury Research Library (CRL)
    See Mingana Collection of
    Middle Eastern Manuscripts
calligraphy 3, 12, 34, 54–55, 99
Cambridge Mosque 125
Cameron, David 72
Cartwright Hall, Bradford
Casey, Louise 73
Charlie Hebdo 115
class 86–87
colonialism 33, 41, 42–3, 51, 94

Colston, Edward 97
Coltrane, John 27
Contemporary Christian Music
   (CCM) 23–27, 29
Cordoba 52
counter-extremism *See* prevent
Courtauld Institute 109
culture 3
cultural exchange 123–124

David Collection, Copenhagen 93
Davis, Angela 34
decolonial/decoloniality 33, 44, 96–98, 122
Def, Mos 2, 23
Desperado (rapper) 72
Du Bois, WEB 88–89

equality policy 6
El-Khairy, Omar 84–87
Elshayyal, Khadijah 41
Eurocentrism 12, 33, 42
Everyday Muslim 8

Fanon, Franz 34
Festival of Muslim Cultures and Ideas 24
Floyd, George 97
fitrah 53–54, 56
Frank, Josefine 101

Gamiet, Ayesha 44
Garvey, Marcus 23
geometric art 35, 116
Gilroy, Paul 2
Ghetts 72
Gramsci, Antonio 27
Grant, Amy 23
Green, Caitlin 124
Grime (music) 13, 68–70, 72–74
Guidance Hub 62–63

Haram Ash-Sharif 52
Hayes, Jefreen M. 125
Heems 73
hijab 40
hip-hop 2, 23, 26, 68–69, 73–74
Hoa Hakananai'a 96
Hodgson, Marshall G. 3
holocaust 88
Homegrown (play) 84–85
hooks, bell 34
Hunt, Tristram 96
Husn (beauty) 55
Hussain, Faisal 8

Ilyas, Tez 24
Index on Censorship 86
integration 72–73
ISIS 85
Islamic art, defining 33, 40, 51–52,
   110–112
Islamic geometry *See* geomatric art
Islamophobia 42, 113–114, 121–122
Islam, Yusuf 5
islimi (biomophic) 33, 36
Issa, Hanan 9

Jazz 2
Jones, LeRoi *See* Baraka, Amiri
Jung, Carl 52

Kano 69
Kasmani, Shaheen 101
Kassim, Sumaya 98
Kesvani, Hussein 7
Khabeer, Suad Abdul 68
Khayaal Theatre Company 9, 24
Khidr Collective 7
King, Martin Luther 28
Komaroff, Lisa 113
Krept and Konan 72
Kweli, Talib 2

Lady Leshurrs 72
Latif, Nadia 84–87
Lings, Martin 38
Los Angeles Contemporary Museum
   of Art 112
Louvre 93

Macron, Emmanuel 95
Malcolm X 2, 23, 25, 28, 34
Maqdala crown 95–96
Manchester Museum 98
Mecca2Medina 2
Me Too (movement) 29
Metropolitan Museum, New York 112
Michelangelo 53
Middle Eastern music 30
Miller, Monica 68
Mingana Collection of Middle Eastern
   Manuscripts 14, 100–105
Moore, Diane 71
Morrison, Toni 23, 45
Mughal Empire 74, 104–105
Museum of Islamic Arts and Heritage
   Foundation, UK 124
Museum of Islamic Art in Berlin 93

Museum of Islamic Art, Doha 93
Museum sector 6, 14, 42, 93–96, 98,
    109, 112, 124; Muslim
    engagement with 98–99, 103
Musical instruments 123
Muslim art and Islamic art 40, 51
Muslim artists 15; experiences of 15
Muslim consciousness 32
Muslims in Britain *See* British Muslim
    community
Muslims in Britain Research
    Network 10

Napoleon (rapper) 5
Nastaliq script 53–54
National Museum of World
    Cultures 96
National Trust 123
National Youth Theatre 84
Nawaz, Aatif 9
Nasr, Seyyed Hossein 4, 36, 51
Newark Congress of African People 23
Ngugi Wa Thiongo 34
Norman, Larry 26

Ogunnaike, Oludamini 4
Orientalism 34, 42, 114
Ottoman Empire 111

Perez, Hamza 2
Pirous, Abdul Djalil 5
prevent/preventing extremism 40–41,
    85, 87
Prophet Muhammed 39, 43
Prothero, Stephen 71
Poetic Pilgrimage 2
poetry 63–64, 99
Pugh, Martin 124

Qaradawi, Yusuf al- 6
Qur'an 3, 14, 42, 99, 101–102, 115

Rahman, Zakiyyah 2
religiosity and art 43–44, 45
religious literacy 71
Redinho 73
Rembrandt 53
Rhodes Must Fall 34, 97
Rifat, Saba 115
Roseby, Paul 85
Roy, Arundhati 34

Rumi's Cave 62–63
Rumi, Jalaluddin 62

Said, Edward 34, 97, 114
Saleem, Shahed 125
Sarr, Felwine 95
Savoy, Bénédicte 95
September 11th 89, 122
Simone, Nina 44
Shahalom, Ali 9
Shahraz, Quaisra 9
Shakur, Assata 34
Shaw, Wendy 122
Skepta 69, 72
Slovo, Gillian 87
social media 63
Spivak, Gayatri 97
Stevens, Cat *See* Islam, Yusuf
Stormzy 69–71
Swet Shop Boys 68, 73–74.
    See also Ahmed, Riz
Sufism 12–13, 42, 58, 59–61, 99; neo-
    and universal 60; poetry
    See poetry; on social media 63
Syed, Soraya 44

tariqa (Sufi order) 58, 60–62, 64
Tawheed 38
theatre 14, 83–84, 87
Tilborgh, Yolanda van 4
Timms, Stephen (MP) 70

Utley, Ebony 68

Victoria and Albert Museum (V&A)
    93–94, 96, 109, 122

War on Terror 41
West, Kanye 70
Why is My Curriculum White 34
Wiley (rapper) 69, 73
Winegar, Jessica 122
women-led arts 9–10, 43
Woodhead, Linda 70–71

Yusuf, Sami 24, 30

Zia, Aisha 8
Zinnenburg, Khadijah von 69
Zuhd (detachment) 55–56

For Product Safety Concerns and Information please contact our EU
representative GPSR@taylorandfrancis.com
Taylor & Francis Verlag GmbH, Kaufingerstraße 24, 80331 München, Germany

www.ingramcontent.com/pod-product-compliance
Lightning Source LLC
Chambersburg PA
CBHW060900170526
45158CB00001B/427

9 781032 362038